STOCK MARKET INVESTING FOR BEGINNERS 101

The Ultimate Guide To Stock Market Investing &
Trading For Beginners - Discover How To Easily
Invest & Make Money Trading Stocks And Dominate
The Market Like A Pro!

Jordan Priesley

TABLE OF CONTENTS

INTRODUCTION

Over the years, people - especially those who have no clue what the stock market is - have looked at it with suspicion. Getting them to invest in the stock market is like trying to sell ice to an Eskimo. It is virtually impossible. The moment you meet them physically or online and want to talk stocks with them, they start giving you one hundred and one reasons why the venture is risky and could collapse at any time. The fluidity of the market doesn't help matters, but like all business, there are always risks involved in trading. What makes a business stand the test of time is to know how to adjust to fit the market environment and demands.

Reading a bunch of articles online, getting books that explain stock broking in a broader sense, watching tutorial videos, and staring at pie charts, bar charts, and all manner of charts without knowing if they are important or not has been the downfall of many people. All you get from putting in so much effort are just bits and pieces of information. If you cannot see the big picture, you are as good as getting stuck in tar. The harder you struggle, the more stuck you get.

To a large extent, life consists of overcoming the problems we encounter in our attempts to achieve our purposes. Along with the easy problems in life are many enormously complex and difficult ones. These would be considerably less difficult if our notions about how the world works were more reliable.

It is comforting to have reliable knowledge to deal with problem and situations situations that have straightforward, linear cause-and-effect relationships. For example, fixing a flashlight that no longer works by replacing the batteries poses little challenge to our knowledge of cause and effect. But, approaching complex problems with an overly simplistic linear mindset often makes matters worse instead of better.

Based on an analysis of the work of people, especially scientists, who have been extremely successful in solving complex problems, I have learned three lessons that are important to a better understanding of knowing:

Reality as we know it is just our perception of it — a kind of map of reality, not the true territory of reality.

Action is an integral part of cause-and-effect loops, with purpose playing a critical - and often overlooked role.

Identifying the strongly held assumptions (beliefs) that influence what we perceive and how we determine our actions in the world is vitally important in opening us up to perceiving new feedback information and to faster knowledge improvement.

Putting these lessons into practice takes conscious effort because much of our life experience has been dealing with the outside world as independent components of reality for which one-way, or linear, cause-and-effect thinking is adequate.

The Loop

The perceiving - acting - knowing system can be visualized as a loop of intimately related components. A useful understanding of how this system functions requires a focus on the loop as a whole and not on the components in isolation.

As noted by the psychologist Hadley Cantril, perceiving, acting, and knowing are interdependent processes. Nevertheless, a discussion of the Loop requires some starting point. For convenience, we will begin at the point where an individual is trying to achieve a purpose within the context of the perceived world "out there."

Purposes

Purposes are personal. They are the outcomes we, as individuals, seek from the actions we take. (This is not to say we always get what we seek.) The great bulk of our purposes are mundane. Consider all the specific, detailed purposes and related actions taken in driving to work — from a small, or low–level, action such as moving the steering wheel a little to the left or right to counteract a crosswind, so the car stays on our intended course. Some larger, or higher-level, purposes of driving to work would include: why you work (survival? self-fulfillment? enjoyment?) and why you have a particular job (steppingstone to a better job? prestige? power?). It quickly becomes evident that we function within a hierarchy of purposes, with higher purposes guiding, or setting lower purposes.

Being cognizant of higher-level purposes is especially relevant to business wealth creation. An example is given of the decision of a Japanese pharmaceutical company's top management to align the firm's mission statement (purpose) with the higher-order purpose of genuinely helping patients that were widely shared by employees. One result was significantly improved corporate financial performance.

Studies of brain activity suggest that many of the common things we do are not associated with brain areas that are responsible for awareness or consciousness. We operate much of the time as if on autopilot (Gazzaniga, Ivry, and Mangun, 2008). This is highly functional, and indeed necessary.

Otherwise, our consciousness would be overwhelmed by minutiae — perceptual noise. Evolution has equipped us to do things much more quickly than we could if everything required conscious mental processing. Many actions would be impossible. Think of all the things that require virtually instantaneous "muscle memory," such as getting out of bed, walking, or typing.

But being on autopilot has its downside, too. Consider two economists given the task or purpose of evaluating whether minimum wage legislation is good or bad for the economy. One economist is a believer in free markets, and the other believes government regulation is necessary to prevent or fix market deficiencies. Because of their core assumptions, they are on different automatic pilot programs, and their expectations are already set to a large degree (Olson, Roese, and Zanna, 1996). The data they choose to consider (and ignore), the periods covered, and the forms of analysis employed for the lower-level research purpose of evaluating the economic impact of minimum wage legislation are most likely to be biased.

Economists (and other inquirers) who have a genuine, higher-level purpose of better understanding cause and effect need to explicitly guard against being guided by their automatic thinking and acting templates. Such researchers would be well served by, at an early stage, explicitly working creatively to overcome the heavy hand of often - unconscious beliefs.

Perceptions

Any discussion of perceptions raises the age-old philosophical question, "What is the reality?" (Madden, 1991). Thinking that there is a pure, independent reality needs to be replaced with the concept that reality is dependent on an individual's experience and current knowledge base, such that each of us is a participant in perceptions of what is "out there." This also helps put into practice one of the hallmark criteria of science, namely, that all knowledge is tentative and subject to revision.

In the 1940s and 1950s, Adelbert Ames Jr. and his

colleagues initiated a paradigm shift away from the view of perception as a passive response to the external environment and toward the view of perception as a process actively carried out by the individual (Bamberger, 2006). Ames was frequently labeled a genius due to his path-breaking research in visual perception at the Dartmouth Eye Institute. Ames and John Dewey often exchanged ideas on Dewey's transactional approach to knowledge as it is related to perception (Cantril, 1960).

The Ames Demonstrations were a series of ingenious laboratory experiments that illustrated the dominating influence of observers' strongly held assumptions. For example, assumptions that floors are level, windows rectangular, bigger is closer, and the like, are particularly strong because of our extensive experience with actions being successful based on the validity of these kinds of assumptions. When an experiment falsifies a strongly held assumption, we nevertheless construct a visual "reality" that conforms to what we "know" to be true.

The Ames Demonstrations in visual perception were instrumental in showing that purpose, perception, and action are all parts of a single connected system. These experiments strongly suggest that perception is never a sure thing, never an absolute revelation of "what is." Rather, what we see is a prediction — our construction designed to give us the best possible bet for carrying out our purposes in action.

We make these bets based on our experience. When we have a great deal of relevant and consistent experience to relate to stimulus patterns the probability of success of our prediction (perception) as a guide to action is extremely high, and we tend to have a feeling of surety. When our experience is limited or inconsistent, the reverse holds. . . .

Perception is a functional affair based on action, experience and probability. The thing perceived is an inseparable part of the function of perceiving, which in turn includes all aspects of the total process of living.

The interdependent processes that contribute to visual perception are analogous to the components of the Loop, which are best viewed as cross-linked together in a system that, for the most part, operates simultaneously as opposed to a mechanistic step-by-step procedure.

It is important to keep in mind when you are investing in the stock market that it functions as a system. Our knowledge base has a significant impact on how we see the world and how we react to situations in the stock market as well as life as a whole. We must remember that knowledge is always incomplete and situations are complex. We can't always simplify and make assumptions based solely on our own individual knowledge bases.

This guide will break everything down into small bits. I won't be going around in a circle. I will strike the nail on the head and make my point as clear as possible.

I will also avoid bringing up equations that would give you a headache. Parts of this guide are designed in a question and answer format. The questions will be probable ones. It is going to be a rich guide that will answer all your questions and prop up the zeal and confidence in you to invest in the stock market.

SECTION 1: STOCK MARKET

THE BASICS OF INVESTING

INVESTING

Simply put, investing is utilizing your money in such a way that it earns more money for you after you have removed the capital and expenditures. Something beautiful about investing is that you know the money is working for you 24 hours a day, seven days a week - and it doesn't get tired. All that money needs is someone who understands it and knows how to invest it in the proper channel.

This section will point out one thing, the art of investing your money in something which may not necessarily be the stock market. Come along; it will get more exciting and expository as we go.

Why should you invest your money?

Inflation is currently the biggest enemy every economy is fighting. In economics, inflation is defined as a general increase in prices of goods and services and a fall in the purchasing value of money. Put in layman's terms, inflation has to do with an increase in the prices of commodities and services we regularly get while the value of money takes a dip. No one and nothing is exempted from the impact of inflation as it hits everything that makes life comfortable.

Goods and services that people bought for a cheaper price years ago are now more expensive due to inflation. The value of $10 in the year 1920, according to The Bureau of Labour Statistics, is worth nearly $120 today. That is over one thousand percent inflation. It shows one thing; it was easier to live on $10 in the year 1920 than it is today. The prices of goods and services valued at that amount increased with time. It shows that the value of $10 and its purchasing power decreased geometrically while the value of the goods and services it can purchase increased.

Inflation is a factor we have no control over, as the price of food, rent, transportation, electricity, cable, and other necessities will continue to climb up the scale. In the same manner, the goods and services purchasable and affordable by $10 will continue to decrease. There is every tendency that $10 of today will be worth a lot in twenty or thirty years. It is an inescapable truth.

What does inflation do?

Inflation, like climate change, does not only affect the lives we are leading now but also our dreams and aspirations for the future. Let's take this simple analogy:

Imagine you are in a race of exchanging batons and at the end when you hand over your baton, you get to choose your dream house, car, or even a vacation. Whether you arrive first or last is ruled out. The important thing is you get the prize as long as you hand over your baton.

You've been in the race for a while now; you are running out of breath and putting every last ounce of your energy into passing the baton. You can see others passing too, at the verge of passing theirs in front of you, while some others are running beside you. Still others gave up and stopped the race halfway, but you keep pushing.

Suddenly, another runner draws your attention. You look at him and he points to the ground. You check only to find out that your shoes became untied in the course of the race. You go down and begin to tie your shoes but immediately notice something; the ground you are on is moving backward.

Confused by this, you put your hand on the ground to inspect more closely. You discover that the ground is moving backward! The movement is slow, but it is moving! You lift your head to confirm if the same thing is happening everywhere. You even take a few steps backward to check it out. After checking it a couple of times, you realize you've wasted time looking at the ground. You spring back up on your feet and enter into the race again. This time, you push yourself harder. You have to get to the finish live.

This analogy describes inflation. We get moved backward, financially, little by little. We all know it exists but choose to ignore it. All we do is work harder for our dreams to become a reality but we don't realize that we get pushed back and farther from achieving our dreams by inflation. If the cost of our dreams today is $250,000, it will cost $290,000 in five years and $350,000 in ten years. In twenty years, it would have tripled.

The good news is this; inflation can be fought! This is by learning how to invest.

Investing – The Sure Way to Fight Inflation

People are continuously divided into two groups by inflation: the investors, who are above inflation, and the "non-investors". The investors who can invest above inflation accumulate wealth and become richer. Those who are scared of investing create poverty and become poor. As unfortunate as it seems, this is the story of a lot of people. They forget that there is a thin line between being poor and being rich and staying rich is investment. Time and consistency is also a determining factor. When you invest constantly, you tend to save more, and inflation doesn't get to you. Not investing and depending on your salary as your only source of income increases your wealth on the negative side, below inflation.

What will happen if you fail to invest?

When you get a 5% increase per year or a 0.4% increase per month or a 0.01% increase in the costs of goods and services, you find it impossible to notice it. So it is safe to say that inflation can be an invisible enemy. You don't get to see its impact on a day to day basis.

Retirement is the portal that opens you up to the full impact of inflation. You realize that having not fought it, you are left at its mercy and have to keep adjusting and re-adjusting until you are swimming in the murky waters of poverty. Since you do not have enough money for failing to invest, your last days are spent financially constrained and a burden to the ones you love the most.

For most organizations and government institutions, the retirement age is pegged at 65 or after 35 years of active service. Now imagine at the age of 65, and you are no longer working. Who pays for your water, food, medicine, electricity, and doctor's visits? Would your pension be able to cover all those mentioned above? Do you see the picture clearly in your mind? No investment, no income coming in, and a lot of expenses waiting to be cleared. A very grim future, if you ask me.

Life expectancy of an average American was pegged at 78.69 years in the year 2016. Now, when you retire at the age of 65, you will need enough funds to keep you going for about 13 or more years. Let's check how much it will cost in estimation. I will be asking some questions which you will answer.

1. How much will you be spending per month if you retire today?

How much would be coming in as your pension after you retire?

Alright, let's peg your current salary at $8000 per

month or $96,000 per year. How many years do you have left before retirement? 15? What's your yearly cost of living? Over $60,000, according to the Bureau of Labour Statistics, is spent annually by an average American family. What do you have left? How much is your pension? Will it be enough to keep you floating when you finally retire?

It is my sincere hope that after answering the questions above, the amount you see ends up scaring you into taking action immediately. You can easily delay investing; you can even go ahead and ignore it, but the tradeoff from your actions at the end of the day is extremely painful.

I work with a good organization that gives me pay raise every year.

Congratulations! I am sure you work hard and are deserving of your yearly pay raise. This doesn't take you away from the need to invest, though. The "money-illusion" as it is called gives you the tendency to think of the money in its absolute amount instead of its purchasing power.

The Money Illusion

Let me tell you a story to buttress this point:

John works for a construction company. Being active with a lot of energy is something that he is proud of. Now, because of his ability, skills, and endurance, he gets a lot of job offers. John also works two to three jobs every day in the same company. He has one for the morning, another for the afternoon, and a third one in the evening.

John earns around $15 in the morning. This he spends on his favorite breakfast which is from KFC. 8 pc. chicken and soda to wash it down. The meal costs him $15, which is just enough.

John got a 10% raise in salary a year later. This increased his pay to $22 daily. John was happy that he would be able to save an extra $7. He was delighted with himself. But check out his surprise when he went to KFC the following morning for his favorite meal. There was also an increase in the price of the chicken and soda bringing everything to a total of $20. John is happy to get a raise, so instead of being turned away by the price, he still goes ahead and makes the purchase. That means reducing his savings to just two dollars.

The above is a perfect example of the absolute amount versus its purchasing power. John got the raise quite all right, but the price of his meal also increased. That means instead of being richer as he had thought he would be with the $7, he only got richer by $2 - which isn't much. John was fortunate to have a raise that is higher than inflation.

A Raise Lower Than the Rise in Inflation

There could be a more upsetting situation at the end of the day, too. This is when inflation jumps higher than the raise in pay given. And unfortunately, for the majority of workers, an annual pay increase does not cover the rising cost of living.

Let's look at another analogy:

We won't be using John again this time. Let's look at James (yeah, James could be the twin brother to John. It is my story). James works in the same company as John, and they are best of buddies (apart from being twins). Both of them earn $15 every morning and both of them always buy their meals from KFC. At just about the same time as John, James got a raise too. However, his wage was increased to $19. It didn't matter to James. A raise is a raise, all the same, so he was happy with the little increment.

James decides to go to KFC with John that day. James also ordered the same meal John ordered. Handing his money to the cashier, he waited for his receipt and meal. Here is the shocker. The cashier goes like this:

"Sir, the KFC. 8 pc. chicken and soda is now $20. You only gave me $15."

James was shocked and flabbergasted. He didn't know that his meal had gotten more expensive. He turned around and back to the cashier before lifting his head and staring at the menu. He looked back at the cash in his hand. He looks back at the menu and back at his hand again. He keeps this going until the man standing right behind him told him to hurry up.

Well, poor James had to make a quick decision. He didn't have enough cash on him, and he didn't want to keep the line waiting. So he did the honorable thing. He placed an order for a side of potato wedges and was ravenous just one hour later.

James! Poor James! His pay raise had made him happy, but not for long. He could no longer afford his meal at KFC. This is because of one thing; his pay raise was lower than inflation. What happened to him wasn't a pay raise in the least bit. What he had was a pay-cut.

Again, this is another perfect example of the money illusion.

Increase in Salary

Well, your salary can only be said to have increased - and it is a true increase if and only if it is higher than inflation. As long as there is no increase in your salary, whenever there is inflation, it means only one thing: a pay-cut!

When inflation jumps by 0.2% and your salary increases by 2.0 percent, you are on track. The effect of inflation will not impact you. Therefore, if there is an increase in your pay/salary over the past years and it has always beaten inflation significantly and on a consistent basis, you have a better chance of fighting inflation. Sadly, this is not the case for the majority.

However, one thing remains critical; preparation for retirement. Most of us have some sort of plan for retirement income – and you may think you have set yourself up for success simply by enrolling in your company's standard retirement plan. You may also be relying on government retirement programming that you've been investing in via taxes for decades. Unfortunately, for many, this does not support the quality of living you deserve after many years of hard work.

But, I save money already. Do I really need to invest?

The major difference here is the power of compounding interest. Consistently adding money to a savings account is a great habit! Say you save $1,000 per month for 25 years. You would have saved $300.000. Your bank may pay a small amount of interest, so you can expect a bit more than that. How long could you live a life you love on a total of $300,000? You've worked hard for decades, and likely had to live quite frugally to set aside such a chunk of change each month. Yet you will likely need to work part time throughout your retirement, or rely on family support or public assistance when the money runs out.

Or… you invest that amount each month in the stock market… Remember, the stock market is a place where you can put your money to work creating more money! So, if we assume an average 10% annual return, you would have over $1.7 MILLION in net worth, ensuring a much different lifestyle than you would have achieved from savings alone. Not only could you retire comfortably without worry of burdening your beloved family - you'd likely have a legacy to leave behind as well. It is likely you could live on dividends alone, allowing your money to continue growing throughout retirement.

How do I start investing when I'm already in debt?

Hold up! You are in debt already, and you're thinking of investing? No! You should not think about investing just yet. Your top priority when you are in debt shouldn't be investing. It should be getting out of debt! This is just because every gain you make will be eaten up by the penalties of being in debt. If you earn 10% with your investment and inflation works against you by 5% per year, then you have won the battle.

But note this, if your debt is from your credit card, know that it is more powerful. It works against you by 40% per year (3% per month). Whoa! Look at the figure! It is eight times stronger and more powerful than inflation! This means that even if your income from investments is up to 40% (this is difficult if you put all factors in place and is also not consistent), you end up with nothing - zilch! Everything goes into servicing the debt. This is why you make getting out of debt first your top priority!

How do I get out of debt?

Here are some of the most important and practical things you can do to get out of debt. Remember, this isn't a complete guide to getting out of debt!

You need to start by tracking your debt, recording what is being borrowed and what you're repaying toward your debt.

A. Always put into the record the amount you pay for your debt and the amount you borrow each month.

B. Cut down on the amount you borrow each month.

C. The amount you pay toward your debt each month should increase.

There is this saying that is popular everywhere, "Stop borrowing; leave the credit card at home and pay cash for everything!"

If you have heard the saying before, what are you doing about it? Are you getting involved? Chances are that you are not doing it yet. One reason for this is because you find it uncomfortable to change your old habits. Here is a piece of advice from me; start with A, follow with B, and then with C.

When you put records down about how much you're borrowing and paying back, its reality forces you to face your debt problem. Well, it is the most important decision and step to take in the right direction. Failure to know how big your problem is and how much you have solved from it can lead to you not solving it at all at the end of the day.

Knowing how much you borrow and pay back every

month, slowly reduce the amount you are borrowing and also slowly increase, bit by bit, the amount you're paying back. If you borrow $150 every month from different people, try as much as you can to borrow $145 or less this month. That is $5 less, but it is a step. Also, slowly increase the amount you pay back at the end of each month. From paying back only $90, put an effort to start paying $93 per month. The changes might look small, but you are already on your way to becoming debt free.

Keeping record will also keep you motivated to change your habits for the better and help you get out of debt faster. As you pay off each debt, you'll experience a rush of pride at the freedom you experience. You will find yourself looking for small ways to save within your daily routine so that you can borrow less that month and pay back more.

By allowing yourself to stay "in the dark" about your debt situation, the problem continues to grow. You may start out not owing much but feeling a despair that keeps you from confronting the issue and leads you to expanding debt and stress. If you are looking to make more money to create a more comfortable future for yourself, the very first step is eliminating your debt so that you have the funds to invest.

Staying Out of Debt!

Avoid leveraging options that may be offered by your bank or brokerage firm. Funds may be offered to help you complete a purchase, usually 50% of the purchase value. Of course, if that stock grows and you are able to cash out at a profit, that's great. But imagine if it falls instead. Now, you've lost money and area also in debt - not just the loaned funds, but interest as well. And of course, should the stock rise, imagine how much sweeter your gains had you used only your own capital to make the purchase.

I'll invest when I'm rich.

A lot of people bring this up as their objection and defense for not investing. It is just plain silly! Saying you will wait until you are rich before you start investing is like saying:

- I will only work harder when I get promoted.

- I will cut my hair when I finally get a girlfriend.

- I promise to give it my all when I get a big break!

We all know one thing; all the promises above always work in reverse.

You only get promoted when you work hard. You get your big break when you give in your all; and finally, you will be rich only when you invest. I don't want to talk about getting a girlfriend as soon as you...

You will not land the better gig by being lazy and waiting for it, with promises of being a better employee once you do. You have to prove your worth in the role you have.

And you will not suddenly become rich without a plan to make your money work for you in the form of investment of some sort. You have to start somewhere, and for many of us, that means starting small and building from there.

Where and how do I invest?

Aside from the stock market, there are many other types of investments available. These investments include, but are not limited to bonds, time-deposits, precious metals, mutual funds, foreign currency, and many more. We will be looking at the most basic ones for now. Keep in mind that you don't have to pick just one as we go through the various investments. It is a widely known fact that successful investors do not put all their money into one investment vehicle. They diversify. But, since this is a startup guide, it would be easy to learn one at a time.

What are…?

- **Time Deposits**

This is a fixed-deposit that cannot be withdrawn for a certain period. Generally, the higher the amount and the longer the period it is kept, the higher the returns gained. Time deposits are useful when it comes to short term wealth. They are almost useless when it comes to wealth building. This is because their returns are always lower than inflation.

- **Bonds**

A bond is one way an institution borrows money. You are essentially lending money to an institution when you purchase a bond. In return for lending money to the institution, you are paid interest during the life of the bond. You are also entitled to the principal amount at the end of the term.

- **Mutual Funds**

This is a method of investing. Mutual funds are not investment vehicles of any sort. Different investors have their money pooled into a single fund. Then an investment occurs. The pooled funds could be put into bonds, equities or even foreign exchange. An expert called a "fund manager" always manages the mutual funds. The benefit here is that diversification is built-in, which reduces your risk.

- **Unit Investment Trust Funds (UITF)**

This is similar to mutual funds in the sense that both are collective schemes that are invested and they are both managed by a fund manager. There are some technical disparities between the two, but it isn't relevant to this discussion at the moment.

- **Equities (the Stock Market)**

A stock market is a place where you can invest in "publicly owned" or listed companies. You become a part-owner of a company by buying shares of stock of that company. You also get to participate in the company's ability to grow and make money as a part owner.

Why should I invest in the stock market?

Two reasons are categorically etched on my mind in answer to this question. The first one is purely an economic reason, while the second revolves around your growth as an investor.

- **Higher Returns**

Historically, the stock market has given higher average returns than bonds and inflations. Let's pick an illustration. Take a look from 20 years ago between the year 1989 and the year 2009; you will notice one thing. The performance of the stock market has outperformed bonds and savings accounts. While the growth of the stock market has been steady and peaked at 14.1% in terms of returns, bonds have a growth of 11.0% while savings accounts plus the interest paid into them have a meager 2.3%.

It is also of high importance to stress this fact; the returns of the stock market are not guaranteed - but left over a long period, the potential for returns is great.

Another reason to put your money into the stock market is the expert partnership. Buying the stock of a company automatically turns you into a part-owner of that corporation. It simply means that whenever the company makes money, you also make money. With a couple of dollars, you can own shares in Amazon, Royal Bank of Scotland, Everi Holdings, and many more.

Last but not least, depending on your country, your income tax at the end of the day is bearable. There are countries where money made on the stock market is not taxed while in other countries, depending on how much stock you buy, you may be taxed - albeit, a small percentage.

1. Increased Flexibility

How much money you choose to invest is up to you. Prices for shares in individual companies range from a few dollars to thousands of dollars. Most mutual funds, on the other hand, have minimums, often of $1,000 or more.

Financial Literacy

This is my favorite reason for encouraging investment in the stock market. You get to grow exponentially as an investor. Your responsibility increases more when you invest in the stock market than when you make a one-time bank deposit. And because of the responsibility involved, you get to learn more. There is a reward for learning more too. You get to earn more!

This is why it is important to me. I have this strong belief that financial literacy is the sole solution to poverty. We get to retain our position as the leading nation economically if every American knows how to manage their money well, how to invest, and ultimately how to create wealth.

STOCK MARKET

While the previous section focused on the "Why" questions, this section will do justice to the "What" and a bit of "How" in the stock market.

What is the stock market?

The stock market is a place where stocks of companies are publicly listed, and from where you can buy and sell shares of stock. I will elaborate on four key terms in the definition I've given:

- **A Place**: It's called a place because of the location. Unlike other countries that have just one stock exchange, The United States has 13 registered stock exchanges operating currently in the United States. But we don't have to visit all of them to trade.

- **Buy and Sell**: This is the reason it is called a stock "market." There are elected representatives who are called "Trading Participants" or brokers. These people can buy and sell stock directly. Individual investors transact with these brokers.

- **Shares of Stock**: Whether called stocks, shares of stock, or shares, they all mean the same the same thing. They represent the ownership of a company. A sole-proprietorship has just a single share which is owned by the founder of the company. However, corporations have multiple shares which can be owned by different people. These are the shares that are bought and sold in the stock market.

- **Companies that are Publicly-Listed**: The stock market does not have all registered corporations on it. Corporations must be publicly listed companies. A company that offers its shares of stock to the public is a publicly-listed company. Listing companies is usually done to put funds into expanding operations. So that the general public can invest, the company must first past strict standards set by the various stock exchanges.

In summary, the stock market is just four things:

- It is a place where (b.) you can buy and sell (c.) Shares of stock in (d.) publicly listed companies.

The stock market is made of exchanges, like the New York Stock Exchange (NYSE) and Nasdaq in the US. Exchanges bring buyers and sellers together and act as a market for the exchange of shares of the company. The exchange also tracks the supply and demand of each stock, which in turn drives the price of the stock. Stocks can't be exchanged at any time – business is conducted only during specific business hours, with some additional before- and after-hours sessions available depending on your broker.

So, how does the stock market work?

In the stock market, there are interactions between

four groups. This interaction makes the stock market work. These groups are the Investors (You), the Trading Participants (Trade Brokers), The Stock Exchange, and the Publicly Listed Companies.

- **The Publicly Listed Company and the SE (Stock Exchange):**An application is forwarded to the Stock Exchange by the publicly listed company so they can be allowed to offer shares of stock to the public. The company is bonded to comply with very stringent requirements before the investments are opened to the public. You, as the investor, are protected by the SE. Your interests are safeguarded.

- **The SE and the Trading Participant (Broker)**: There is no direct transaction between the SE and us the investors. The only people allowed to have direct transactions are the Trading Participants. They buy and sell shares of stock. This act was enacted simply for control purposes and making work simpler. The SE makes it its priority to monitor Publicly Listed Companies while the Trading Participants deal with the investing public.

- **The Trading Participant and the Investor (You!)**: If you wish to buy or sell shares, you will have to contact a trading participant or broker. To help you do this, a broker will charge a nominal amount for fees for the buying or selling transaction. Information is also provided to you by the brokers on which companies are good to buy in addition to their transaction services.

To recap, this is how the Stock Market works: (a.) Companies who want to be publicly listed are monitored and screened by the SE. (b.) Trading Participants are assigned by the SE to interact with the public for the buying and selling of shares. (c.) Trading Participants become the middlemen between the SE and the investing public.

How do I make money in the Stock Market?

Have this in mind; investing in the stock market is buying ownership of businesses. That means you make money the same way its business owners make money. You do this through dividends and capital gains.

- **Dividends**

  Your share of earnings in the company as an investor is the dividends. If a company declares its dividends, it means one thing; they are also shareholders and are paying themselves too. That means, there is a joint partnership between you and the company. You get paid the same way they do too.

  Dividends can be paid in cash (which we then encourage you to invest into the market to capitalize your earnings further) or in additional shares paid out to shareholders in lieu of cash.

- **Capital Appreciation or Capital Gains**

  The second way to make money in the stock market is through capital appreciation. This means that the value of the company grows and is worth more than when you bought your shares.

How much money can be made in the stock market?

A percentage of the amount of money you put into the stock market is what you can gain or lose. Your willingness to learn and become disciplined in applying what you learn can affect how high or low this percentage is. Before I delve into some personal details and start calling out numbers, it is important you know that whether a percentage is high or low, it is often compared to the market average.

For instance, I had a 30% gain in the year 2011. Well, 2011 was a very good year, so I personally think this is a good average. In one of the seminars I attended, a member of the audience was asked how much money he had made in his stock trading. His answer was amazing. A hundred percent! He doubled his money in just one year. Beautiful!

This may, however, not have been the same in the year 2008 during the time of financial crisis and economic meltdowns everywhere. The average returns were negative! It means if an investor had made profit, his performance is considered above average.

Isn't the stock market risky?

It is. It is very risky. You will also be dealing with two kinds of risk: inherent risk due to market capitalization and risk due to ignorance.

- **Inherent Risk Due to Market Capitalization**

This is a risk because you cannot, at any given time, predict the price of a stock 100%. One of the things that guide forecasting (a process of making intelligent predictions) is that a more short-term, specific prediction has a higher chance of being wrong. The opposite is also true of this matter; the more general predictions have a higher probability to be correct.

This means that if there is a prediction that there will be an increase in the price of the stock by 10%, this week, it is very likely for it to turn out wrong when compared to a prediction that says the price of the stock would have increased by 10% over the next two years. That is why it is riskier to invest in the short term than investing for the long term. The stock market has this risky status because you cannot successfully predict the exact value of your investment. When you acknowledge that the prediction of your exact stock could be wrong, you find the amount of risk is acceptable. You can easily manage this risk by diversifying your stocks and putting in place other investment strategies.

However, when the investor assumes that his prediction may turn out correct, the inherent risk automatically becomes a huge problem. After he had settled for his prediction, the investor will be likely unprepared for the events that may unfold if he turns out wrong. This risk is a very dangerous one, and you should be aware and wary of it. The risk is due to ignorance.

- **Risk due to Ignorance**

I have a favorite quote on investing. This quote is largely underrated though. It states that, "It's not the investment that is risky... It's the investor".

When you fully grasp this quote made by Robert Kiyosaki, you will understand that investments can have little or no risk. When the investor ends up not being able to tell the difference, the risk comes. The above quote confused me when I first read it. It took me reading it over and over again to grasp it fully. This is because it challenged one of the oldest principles in investment: "High risk, high return."

This means if Roberto Kiyosaki turns out to be right, it is possible to earn higher returns, without having to take on higher risks. You only need to become a smarter investor. This is both confusing and empowering at the same time. Upon further study, I fell across this passage from the book *The Intelligent Investor*:

"It has been an old and sound principle that those who cannot afford to take risks should be content with a relatively low return on their invested funds. From this, there has developed the general notion that the rate of return with which the investor should aim for is more or less proportionate to the degree of risk he is ready to run. Our view is different. **The rate of return sought should be dependent, rather on the amount of intelligent effort the investor is willing and able to bring to bear on his task. The minimum returns go to our passive investor, who wants both safety and freedom from concern. The maximum return would be realized by the alert and enterprising investor who exercises maximum intelligence and skill."**

Benjamin Graham (The Intelligent Investor)

Reading this, especially the text emboldened, made me feel great. I felt great because I realized that there is no dependency on the success in the stock market on chance. It depended on disciplined study rather.

Overall, the risks of investing in the stock market is dramatized. There are some people who suffer big losses with severe consequences. However, the majority of investors have found safe strategies that reduce the risks. As with all subjects, the media reports only the extremes in market fluctuation.

Keep in mind that investments in the stock market are meant to be long-term. One financial expert, Dave Ramsey, says, "The only people who get hurt riding a roller coaster are the ones that jump off." Simply put, if you panic and sell off when there is a temporary drop in the price of your stocks, you face the biggest risk. You have to keep in mind the long-term.

Understand Your Risk Tolerance

We all vary in our tolerance to risk. This tolerance is influenced by genetics, education, income, wealth, and age and refers to how much you can psychologically stand to risk. Risk tolerance is also affected by our perception of how risky an action is. For some, riding on an airplane may be perceived as having a high risk, while for others, riding the subway may incite more anxiety. Finances can be very personal for some of us and can create very strong emotional responses. It is important to know what your limits are in terms of how much you can invest and the types of risks you are able to tolerate so that you don't set yourself up a stress-filled investment experience.

How much money do I put in the stock market?

As an average investor, the money you should put into the stock market is money that you won't need today, tomorrow, next year, or in five or even ten years. The reason is this; you cannot and can never exactly predict the value that your investment will turn out to hold in the coming years. So, even as I stated earlier that the average return the stock market had from 1989 to 2009 was 14% per year, future returns are never exactly guaranteed.

It is also recommended that you don't purchase all of your stock at once. If you're planning a purchase, split this up into three amounts and purchase shares 30 days apart. This way, you reduce some of your risk and build confidence in your abilities to choose the best companies to invest in.

The Biggest Problem with Investing

I don't know how this may sound to you, but I will say it anyway. The biggest problem that can spring up in investment is when some personal problems or challenges of yours force you to suddenly sell off your investments for cash when the market is down.

Let's take the story of Danny, for example. He invested all of his savings – reaching up to $5600 in the stock market. He hoped that someday, the money would serve as a down payment for a house. Unfortunately, there was an accident. The bones in his left leg were crushed. To get his legs fixed and on the road to total recovery would cause him around $5600. Even though the company Danny works for offers benefits for medical incidences, his employer could only pay $1000. That leaves Danny to find a way to pay for his share of the treatment which amounts to $4600. The stock market is the only place Danny had money. Unluckily, it was a down market, and the value of his investment was just $4600.

This didn't surprise Danny one bit. It had happened in the past. The value of stocks would plunge down and then it would shoot up again. Normally, Danny waited it out. But not this time. He just couldn't afford to wait for the values to climb up again before paying his hospital bills. So, he went ahead and withdrew his investment worth $4600 - which is taking a loss of $1000.

This is one among the list of discouraging things that can happen when you put all your money in the stock market.

Make sure this doesn't happen to you!

You can use one of the three ways I will list below to prevent the problem above and protect your investment whenever there is a sudden need for cash. Before you invest in the stock market, I strongly recommend that you do all of them.

- **Be Insured:** Yes, get insurance that will cover you in the case of accidents (it could be you in it, your loved ones, your car, your home or your business). The insurance company will be obligated to pay for damages, and at the same time, there would be no need for taking money out of your investments to fix things.

- **Keep aside an emergency fund**: Emergency funds are sums of money kept aside in the case of an emergency. The cash that should be kept aside should total six months of your total yearly living expenses. There may be incidences in your life which are unplanned or won't be covered by insurance. For example, if you lose your job, there are funds to survive on before the next job comes along.

- **Remember to only put in money you won't**

need for a very long time: For you to be able to do that, you have to have a very good grasp of the amount you will be spend. And remember to always remove the once-a-year expenses like birthdays and holidays. You may find it tempting to touch your investments if the 13th-month salary isn't enough for your Christmas expenses.

Investing in the stock market is a marathon, not a sprint!

I can't emphasize this enough! ONLY INVEST MONEY YOU WON'T NEED for several years. Longevity of investment is where the money is made. If you are constantly investing and then cashing out when you find yourself low on readily-available funds to meet your immediate needs, you will be in a constant state of stress. You will also continuously lose money if you're withdrawing money at inopportune times. It can be difficult to determine a good balance between setting money aside in investment for the future and ensuring you have all that you need while you wait for it to grow. Developing a detailed budget will be helpful here.

How much time do I need to spend doing it?

This is wholly dependent on you and your investment strategy. Some people go through their portfolio once in a while in such a way that if the total time is calculated, it amounts to one hour per year. Others check it so frequently that it sums up to up to eight hours per day! Now that is a bit much.

When one of my friends started, he always took the time to look at his portfolio every hour. It was exciting to him watching and seeing how his money went up and horrifying to see the same thing go down. He kept checking it out even though he didn't "do" anything with it. His habit only lasted for about two weeks before he got used to it. Now, seeing his money on either +15% or -15% doesn't matter much to him anymore. He came to realize that checking it frequently is boring and, well, a waste of time.

What does he do now? He just spends up to twenty or thirty minutes every other Saturday or Sunday to read up his stocks. And at the end of every month, he spends a little more time to place his buy orders in the stock market. He spends more time studying the stock market now than simply gawking at the figures at his portfolio and illogically cheering it on.

Do you know what my friend's story shows? It is this: there is little or no relationship between the amount of time spent "buying and selling' and the amount you can make in the stock market. Instead, the amount of money you will make is proportional to how much the quality of what you have learned is being applied.

The Millionaire Next Door is a bestselling book by Thomas Stanley, Ph.D. and William Danko. The book studied the lifestyles of the wealthiest men in America. Over 500 millionaires and over 11,000 high-net-worth and high-income individuals were interviewed by the duo. Questions asked about ranged from their cars, suits, shoes, vacations, houses, worries, and much more. And most importantly, they asked about how long they kept investments in a specific company. This is what they found out:

a. 90% of millionaire investors are not active traders in the market:

A great number of them hold their stocks for a minimum of one year. An even higher number of the majority holds their stock for a minimum of 6 years or more.

b. Billionaires take their time to study far fewer offerings (companies):

This has made it possible for them to focus their time and energy to master their comprehension of a much smaller variety of offerings in the market.

We suggest not being overly active in trading. Remember, this is a marathon, not a sprint. Stock market investments are meant to be long-term. You by no means need to check on your stocks daily. Checking them quarterly, when you receive your reports, is plenty. Daily review increases your stress level and may keep you focused on the share price rather than the value of the company, which of course is the most important.

Do I have to have millions already before I can start investing?

The answer is no! With extensive use of the internet, you can start investing for as low as $100. The major limitation of the past was that you needed a stockbroker that is personal to you to be able to invest. So a minimum amount of investments were set by the stockbrokers who had limited time before they accepted individual investors. But today, there are stockbrokers online who allow you to invest in the stock market on your own and in your way. All that is needed is a computer and an internet connection that is stable. It is that easy as you can send your buy or sell orders online. The minimum starting amount is much lower because you don't go through the hassle of meeting and talking with a live person.

Here are websites where you can find some of these online brokers. It is expedient to have it in mind that this list is not complete.

Online Stock Brokers

BPI Securities Corporation - www.bpitrade.com

Merrill Edge - www.merrilledge.com

E Trade - www.us.etrade.com

TD Ameritrade - www.tdameritrade.com

COL Financial Inc. - www.colfinancial.com

First Metro Securities Brokerage Corporation - www.firstmetrosec.com.ph

I make use of *CitisecOnline*. No one is paying me to promote them. Being a satisfied customer, I highly recommend them. They have one of the largest online brokerages in the world. They are also one of the very active ones when it comes to promoting stock market education. Introductory stock market seminars are held every week at their office. That's to show you how customer-focused they are.

Won't this be stressful?

There is a high relation between stress and risk. One cannot do without the other. (See the answer to 'Isn't the stock market risky?'). A risky investor is a stressed investor. Stress comes as a result of the feeling of being out of control, and not knowing what next to do. And not knowing what to do next is simply caused by a lack of information. This is caused by a lack of research.

Imagine the scenario of two college students taking a Calculus exam. Student 1 studied several weeks before the exam. Student 2 just started studying the night before. Who do you think would have to deal with more stress before, during, and after the exam?

Now let's turn the example around and use it in the stock market. Josh just heard the news that his officemate, Jake just made $1200 in one day from the stock market. He went ahead and asked a friend for more information. This will let him in on the next big thing on the stock market. A couple of days later his friend tells Josh to put his investment in ABC Company so that could double his money in a week. Josh gets excited over the news, and on the same day, invests his $3000 savings into ABC.

Josh looks at his account the next day and what is left of his money is just $2,800. He turns to his friend and demands an explanation from him. His friend laughs at him and explains in few words that it will recover and that it's a natural phenomenon that occurs. His friend advises Josh to take a look at his account in a week when it's already doubled. Josh being very trusting follows the advice. A week later, he goes back to his account…. And zap! Account Balance: $300. That is 90% of his savings gone like that in one week.

Just think about the stress Josh was going through. He put all of the blame on his friend for losing his money and promised that he would never put his money as an investment in the stock market again. Josh was unprepared and took on a lot of risk due to ignorance. Now, we all know he won't be able to sleep at night because of the stress.

So prepare very well if you don't want the stress. It's that simple.

I am not smart enough! It is just too complicated!

It's just new. It's not complicated, so take it one step at a time. A lot of people think that it is complicated, and because I already know it, I think it's easy. So to see if it's complicated, I ran a little experiment.

I clicked and logged on to my online account, and ran through all the terms a 5th grader probably won't understand. I also went ahead and counted the number of click you had to make for the basic transactions.

Then, I discovered that, of the 90 new terms which will be shown to you when you start investing, you'll only have to remember 32 of them. The rest of the terms aren't really important. This is just like the buttons in your TV/DVD remote. Count the number of buttons available in your TV remote, and then count how many of those buttons you use. Our TV remote has 49 buttons, but I just use 5 of those buttons: Power, Channel Up, Channel Down, Volume Up and Volume Down. If I show our TV remote to a person who has never seen one before, I'm sure they'll also say it's very complicated.

After you finish reading this guide, you'll be able to understand all of those 32 terms, plus a little bit more. And once you buy your first stock, you'll realize how simple it is, what you see when you open the order window. What's important for your first buy?

GETTING STARTED

How do I start investing in the stock market?

There are three ways to get your money into the stock market. The key here is to find which best fits your desired style of investing.

a. Through a Mutual Fund (Equity Funds)

A Mutual Fund is a type of investment wherein the money is pooled from many investors. These funds are professionally handled by the fund manager. Since there are several types of mutual funds, what you should look for is an "Equity Fund," or a fund that has a percentage of it invested in the stock market.

In a mutual fund, you are not buying a specific company. Instead, what you are buying are shares of that specific fund. So if the fund is invested in 10 different companies, your money is also invested in those ten different companies. This also means that you no longer have to decide which companies' stocks to buy and when to sell them. That responsibility is delegated to the fund manager. So if convenience is what you're after, an equity mutual fund may be for you.

b. Through a Traditional Stockbroker

A traditional stockbroker is a living, breathing person who is licensed to give you professional advice on your investments. The good thing about this is that you can get counsel specifically tailored to your investing needs, your investment goals, your timeline, and your tolerance to risk. A good stock broker will be able to advise you on what to buy and when to sell - and notify you of the upcoming opportunities. You can even assign some brokers to manage your portfolio for you while you go on vacation.

The many personalized services that come with this method entail a price – commonly in the form of higher commission rates and higher minimums for starting an account.

c. Through an Online Stock Broker

Investing through an online stockbroker is like being your own stockbroker. On your own, you will be able to buy and sell stocks as long as you have a computer with access to the Internet. Since everything is do-it-yourself, you will be paying the lowest commission rate possible (0.25%).

As for market tips and advice, your online broker would be providing you with tons of reports and market information. It would be up to you how to understand it and how to get the relevant details.

COL Financial, the online broker that I'm using, even created a short-list of companies which they highly recommend to their clients. They call it the Easy-Investment-Program or EIP. I'll talk about this later.

Which among the three options should I choose?

Among these three options, what I generally recommend to starting investors is to start with an online stock broker. Here are the reasons why:

- The minimum amount to start is just $15. This makes it accessible to almost anyone who has a steady source of income. New investors most likely haven't amassed the wealth required to get a full-service broker.

- You're on your own. You will read the company reports. You will decide which companies to buy, and which companies to sell. You will execute your buy and sell orders. You will manage your portfolio. This means you stand to earn the biggest amount. And because you're the one doing everything, you get the biggest advantage.

- You learn everything. This is the number-one reason why I would recommend doing it on your own first, before getting a mutual fund. In a mutual fund, everything is managed for you. Your only responsibility is to write a check or make a deposit to the mutual fund company. (Developing the skill of writing a check and paying someone is very dangerous!). In effect, you're putting up all the capital, but taking none of the responsibility. From a business perspective, that's very risky.

I hope you don't misunderstand. I'm not saying that you shouldn't invest in mutual funds. I also have investments in mutual funds. But if you want to become a good investor, you'll learn much faster when you're doing it on your own.

How do I pick a stockbroker?

A couple of things you should consider when selecting a stockbroker are the following:

- **Broker's Fees:**

For every transaction you make, the broker will get a certain percentage of that amount. The lowest that is allowable by the PSE is 0.25% of the transaction value.

There are other fees which are mandatory such as VAT, PSE Transaction Fees, SCCP, and Sales Tax. These other fees, however, would not vary from broker to broker.

- **Market Information Available:**

The professional (non-generic) information and advice provided to you is the justification for why brokers charge higher than 0.25%. This is why with online brokers (where only generic market information is provided), they charge the minimum.

- **Trust, Reputation, and Stability:**

It is very important that you ensure your broker is registered with the Philippine Stock Exchange and is not a scam. Here is a complete list of online and traditional brokers registered with the PSE. (Broker Directory). A ranking report by volume of transactions is also available in that link.

- **DRIPs (Dividend Reinvestment Programs)**

Some brokers offer programs that automatically take the dividends   paid to you and reinvest them by purchasing more shares of that   stock for you. If you let this run over time, you can have significantly   greater earnings as the dividends will capitalize over time.

Overall, you should pick a broker who matches your investing needs. As a beginning investor with little starting capital, it would be best to pick brokers with the lowest fees. This way, more of your available money is put into stocks rather than transaction fees.

Take the Leap - Quick Tip!

There's no need to waste time picking and researching brokers. Just choose CitisecOnline (COLFinancial.com). They have the lowest fees. It's very easy to invest with them, and they provide a lot of market information. They are one of the largest online brokerage in the world, offering you a higher level of stability in the investment community.

Another option is Ally (formerly TradeKing). There is no minimum initial deposit to open an investment account. And the site offers low fees for purchasing stocks. They are ranked number one on comparebroker.com among accounts with no minimums.

INVESTMENT STRATEGIES

In this section, you'll learn about the different options you have for investing in the stock market. Some are simple, while some are a little more complicated. Take a look at which one would be best for you.

<u>What are the common investing methods?</u>

There are three basic methods of investing: (1) Buy and Hold, (2) Dollar Cost Averaging and (3) Market Timing (or trading). Here you'll learn about each one and why it works.

1. Buy and Hold

The buy and hold strategy is buying a stock and holding onto it until the end of time (meaning, until you want/need to get the money). This strategy is relatively stress-free since you'll be ignoring the daily/weekly/monthly ups and downs of the market. This can be done when you have a sum of money that you don't need now or later in the future – but you just want it off your hands. The important thing here is that you're not attached to the money. If it gets bigger, great! But if it gets lost, then you should still be okay.

With a buy and hold strategy, it's best to pick the giants of today's industry. Pick the companies that will most probably outlive you. These are the companies that have a history of expanding into new ways of making money. Here are some examples:

o   PLDT, the leading Philippines network provider, used to be known only as a provider of telephone services. Then they expanded their business to also provide internet and cellular services. Much more recently, they even acquired a competitor, Sun Cellular.

o   Jollibee Foods Corporation, also in the Philippines, began by just selling Ice Cream. Then the business shifted to selling hot dogs. After the hotdogs, came the Yumburgers and

Chickenjoy. When they couldn't sell any more chicken, they bought Greenwich. This marked their entrance in the pizza-pasta business. Now they own Chowking, Red Ribbon, and Burger King Philippines. And I'm sure you've heard the news that they purchased Mang Inasal.

o San Miguel Corporation, in the Philippines has been recognized for its world-famous San Miguel Beer. But aside from this product, SMC has had a history of expanding into new businesses. Some of these businesses are Meralco, Philippine Airlines and Petron Corporation. San Miguel Corporation will keep on evolving to thrive in the ever-changing market.

A Word of Caution: There is no guarantee that investing in these same

companies today will yield the same returns 11 years from now. If it was the year 2009 – and you had put your money in San Miguel Corporation, your returns would have been negative in 2012.

1. Dollar Cost Averaging

The dollar cost averaging method is a simple, safe, and effective way to make money in the stock market. However, it requires more discipline than the buy and hold strategy. The dollar cost averaging strategy is investing a fixed amount of money in a good company at fixed intervals, regardless of its price. This way, you spread out the risk of buying at high prices, and at the same time take advantage of the opportunities at low prices.

Dollar Cost Averaging is discussed at length in Benjamin Graham's book, *The Intelligent Investor*, which Warren Buffett called "by the far the best book on investing ever written." It has been a guide many successful investors have trusted for years.

Because you're able to purchase more shares when the price is low, the weight of the lower prices is greater. As a result, the average purchase price also goes lower. This is the magic of dollar cost averaging. By buying at fixed intervals, with fixed amounts of money, you take advantage of the price fluctuations. Because you are always invested, you will not be devastated by the losses inherent in trying to time the market, which can be difficult.

Say, for example, you are buying $500 every month in stock using this strategy. The first month, the stock price is $10. You're able to buy 50 shares. The next month, the stock price is $5. Rather than becoming upset and looking for an exit strategy that might leave you with a 50% loss, you instead revel in the ability to buy 100 shares. You'll now have 150 shares in a company whose stock price will likely rise once again. Plus, you've saved yourself a great deal of stress by trusting in a strategy designed by investment giants.

2. Market Timing

Market timing is also known as stock trading. This means actively watching the stock market for opportunities to buy at the lows and sell at the highs. Market timing requires more skill, time and dedication. At the same time, it is also a lot more exciting.

If you're willing to check on the stock market daily, and you want the excitement, this may be for you. With timing the market, you can double your money in a week! But at the same time, the reverse could happen. You could also lose half your money in that same week if you're not careful. This rush of winning and losing is the reason that the stock market is often likened to gambling.

While the concept of buying at the lows and selling at the highs seem simple, it requires knowledge of a science called technical analysis. Technical analysis is a technique where you observe patterns in the stock charts and look for different market indicators. You also can fall victim to bad advice from "investment psychics," and experience more overall stress from attempting to track your investments through the ups and downs and rushing to buy and sell at "just the right times."

Take the Leap - Quick Tip!

Of these three strategies, the best strategy for the new investor is peso cost averaging. You don't need to have huge amounts of capital. You spread your risk. You only need to check on it once or twice a month. It's best for a long-term investment.

If you already have a huge amount of money set-aside (say, P100, 000 and above), divide that portion into 6 portions (or so) and slowly invest it into the stock market using the peso-cost averaging.

CAN SLIM Investing System

There are as many investment strategies as there are investors. One that has worked well for many is the CAN SLIM system. CAN SLIM serves as an acronym for a set of rules to follow.

Current Quarterly Earnings - Watch for stocks that are showing increases in their quarterly earnings of 25% or more.

Annual Earnings Growth - Great companies show growth in annual earnings of at least 25% for at least three years.

New Product, Service, Management, or Price High - Most of the companies who are performing best have something new to offer that consumers can't find anywhere else. Think of the incredible booms Apple experienced upon release of the original iPhone and iPad. These products were limited and pushed the limits of technology. Technological advances are often great investment opportunities.

Supply and Demand - When shares are limited, prices increase. The concept of supply and demand in stock broking is consistent with those in consumer economics in general.

Leader or Laggard - Buy from those who are leading the way in their respective industries. You'll be able to expect innovation and building stock values.

Institutional Sponsorship - Follow the moves of the professional investors managing large portfolios, like mutual funds and pension funds. These investments make up 75% of market activity. Observing closely the choices made by professionals will benefit your own personal portfolio.

Market Direction - Studies show that 3 of four stocks follow the trend of the market at large, so tracking trends will lead you to making the best investment choices.

How do I know which companies to invest in?

The first thing to keep in mind when choosing which companies to invest in is that you're buying a share of the company - which means you're becoming a part owner. So, you need to look at the business as a whole. Don't just focus on the symbols on the ticker. Think of the company. Is this a company you want to be a part-owner of? This is the number-one question to consider.

Why is this a company you're committed to? Keep that in mind - and write it down to review when you're feeling particularly panicky. Think ahead about what might cause you to sell the stocks. When you think about dissolving the investment, look back at those reasons. Is it time to let go, or are you acting rashly?

Professionals use two approaches in deciding which companies to buy stock in: fundamental analysis and technical analysis. Before I explain these two methods, please be reminded that the people who do it are professionals, meaning they spend the majority of their workweek performing these kinds of analyses.

Now, rest assured that you do not need to learn how to do this. I'm just discussing it here so that you have an idea of how it's done. (In the next section, I'll be sharing with you a very practical and convenient way of investing wherein you can leverage on the expertise of these professionals.)

Fundamental Analysis

Fundamental analysis is a technique that estimates the potential value of a stock by focusing on underlying factors that affect a company's business and its future growth. The approach is usually made in a top-down manner, from general to specific. The following example I'll be giving is extremely broad. Don't get scared or overwhelmed, since you don't need to do this. I'm just sharing it so you understand the depth of this technique. The following list is the series of questions one would need to answer using the fundamental analysis approach on a global level.

- Which region is growing? Europe? North America? Asia?

- Which countries in that region have the highest potential for growth?

- Which industries in that country drive the growth?

- Which companies are the leaders in those industries?

- Will these companies continue to be leaders in their industries?

Again, don't worry, because you don't need to do this when you start investing. When I was just starting to study how to invest in the stock market, this was one of the first things that I read; and it overwhelmed me! I felt like I had to read my book from Econ 101 again! (I was supposed to say

"Econ 101 notes" but then I remembered that I didn't take down notes when I was in college!)

Fundamental Analysis: Simpler Version

To make fundamental analysis easier, the best first step is to start with what you already know. Start by identifying the products that you already use and find out who makes them. You'll be surprised that the makers of those products and services are listed in the stock market.

Which fast food restaurants do you eat in? - Take a

look and see if it's owned by TriCorp.

Do you use natural gas? (Of course, you do) - Find out more about Consumer's Energy.

Do you have cable or Internet service? - Look into AT&T or Comcast.

Where do you shop? (Likely the company is listed on the stock market.)

What banks do you go to? Which airlines do you use for travel? Where do you work? If you closely take a look at all of the things you use, you'll have multiple companies with which you can start your research.

A good rule of thumb is to invest in companies that you are familiar with. Think of those companies that came to mind above. You know the products and services they offer. You know how relatively successful they are. All of these things create additional confidence as you invest.

For each of these companies, your goal is to find evidence that these companies will continue to grow in the future. If you can't find any evidence, then don't put your money in it. The more evidence you have, the better your chance of making a good choice.

Which can convince you to buy a stock?

The following list contains examples of "evidence" which you could encounter when studying these companies. As you go through the list, you'll observe that there are pieces of evidence which you'll find ridiculous. I've put them there because there are people who buy stocks based on it. Also, you'll find these ridiculous statements slowly turn into possibly reasonable ones with a few changes.

Which are good enough reasons for you to buy a stock?

- The market share of company XYZ's major product A increased by 10%.

- The net profit of Company XYZ increased by 10% this year.

- Company XYZ's net profit has been growing consistently for the past ten years.

- A guy on the road who was randomly interviewed on TV said, "There are too many condos here in Metro Manila! I don't even know anyone who buys them."

- A guy on the road, dressed in a suit who was randomly interviewed on TV said, "I can afford those condos. But I've never considered buying them."

- A professor of economics who was being interviewed on TV said, "There are already too many condos in Metro Manila. I don't know why these developers are still building them."

- A representative of Ayala during an interview said, "Our research shows that there is a lot of demand for condominiums. Come 2015, all these units would be sold out. So it would be best to buy them now as they're pre-selling at a discounted price."

- My boss just invested $10 million into company XYZ!

- My boss, who is well connected with other investors just invested in company XYZ!

- My boss, whose wife is a mutual fund manager of an international bank, just invested P10m into company XYZ!

As you do your research, you'll be able to uncover a lot of information. Some will make sense while others won't. Some evidence will be based on ten years of performance, while some will be based on the latest rumors. In the end, it will be up to you to decide - because it's your money that will be at stake.

Different Types of Investment:

- **Growth investing** takes advantage of new medical breakthroughs or technologies released by strong companies. You leave room for growth and these investments tend to have a high profit to earnings ratio.

- **Value investing** involves buying stock in companies who have been on a downturn but can be turned around with better management to become a more profitable company. This takes a little faith and a little knowledge of business potential.

- **ProActive Investing** is a combination of the two types above, using options to reduce the cost of the purchase and create revenue during the dreaded wait-time.

Technical Analysis

Technical Analysis is a technique which estimates the future value of a stock by reviewing historical price charts and patterns. The major assumption in technical analysis is that everything that has happened and is happening is already factored into the stock price. And therefore, by studying the stock price alone, you have already factored in everything that could affect the price including fundamental factors and the market psychology.

In short, you only consider the price of the stock with technical analysis. This is in contrast with fundamental analysis where everything seems like a factor to consider. This makes technical analysis look a lot simpler, making more people want to try it out. The dangerous thing is that it's not that simple and it would take more than reading a few articles on the Internet to learn this skill. The seminars on this (offered by CitisecOnline) have two sessions, each one going for at least 4 hours.

I have decided to end the discussion on technical analysis here. The reason is that I do not want to encourage you to try it without more in-depth training.

At this point, it is enough that you know that Technical Analysis exists. Now, if you want to learn more, I've provided references in the last section of this guide.

Fundamental and technical analysis seem like a lot of work! Is there another way?

Yes, there is a better, easier, safer, and more effective way to do it!

It's to learn from experts. Isaac Newton, one of the most influential scientists of all time said, "If I have seen further, it is by standing on the shoulders of giants." So, even though you're new to the stock market, if you look up and follow the experts, you can get good returns in the stock market. At the same time, you will be able to learn a lot because you're still the one responsible for managing your money.

I call this method "Practical Investing." And I love it because it's the way the majority of people (especially those who don't have time) can safely and profitably invest in the Stock Market.

PRACTICAL INVESTING

Practical Investing is a method of investing wherein you simply follow a stock recommendation list given by experts in the Stock Market. This way you get to leverage their time and talent when it comes to choosing stocks.

Who are these experts that can guide me in my investing?

There are a lot of sources online wherein you can get this guidance. A few are great, some are okay, and many are just plain risky. So to answer this question, I will just recommend the best one. I believe that this expert is the best because of the consistency, reliability, integrity, and ease of use.

The Best Source: Bo Sanchez's Stocks Update

Bo Sanchez is the author of the best-selling book, *My Maid Invests in the Stock Market*. Bo Sanchez taught his maids and drivers how to invest in the stock market. The latest news that I read was that his maid already had P100, 000+ in her portfolio. (Yes, he's that good at teaching the stock market.) Bo's motto was that if he could teach his maids how to invest in the stock market, he could teach it to anyone! So, when he already mastered making the stock market simple and easy, he created the "StocksUpdate."

The Stocks Update is a 5-7 page article which contains stock recommendations and the reasons why that company is being recommended. The best part is that it answers the four most important questions you'll have as a stock market investor:

- **What company should I buy?**

- **At what price should I buy it?**

- **When should I sell it?**

Learn and Earn at the Same Time

By the way, did you notice that I said there were

four questions, but only gave you 3? Well, here's the last one. The last and most important question that should be asked by an investor is:

- **Why?**

In the StocksUpdate, the "why" is answered by providing you updates on those recommended companies. You get to learn about the company's net income, expansion plans, growth targets, assets and liabilities, and other relevant financial information.

How were the recommendations in the StocksUpdate made?

It's a combination of fundamental as well as some technical analysis. The specific steps, however, are not publicly available. However, this stock recommendation list is considered to be best because of the minds that created it.

The Stocks Update Mastermind

The "mastermind" of the StocksUpdate is not Bo Sanchez, but his good friend and mentor Edward Lee. Edward Lee is not that popular to the average Filipino, but in the world of the stock market, he's a giant.

Edward was introduced to the stock market at the very young age of 18. And at that time, he was fascinated by it and even borrowed other people's money to invest in it. One year later, the stock market crashed, and he was completely wiped out. He was even buried in debt because he used borrowed money for investing!

But, thankfully for all of us, that stock market crash taught him a lesson. He persevered, recovered, and continued studying and investing in the stock market. Today (35+ years later), he is a stock market giant. He's the founder of COLFinancial, the online broker that I'm recommending to you; and he is also a self-made billionaire! (Yes, with a B!)

Standing on the Shoulders of 2 Giants

The best way to look at the StocksUpdate, then, is to see it as a product of 2 giants: Edward Lee, the stock market genius, and Bo Sanchez, the brilliant and inspiring motivational speaker.

Edward Lee provides the technical expertise of the recommendations. Then, Bo Sanchez translates the recommendations into a simple and entertaining manner in the StocksUpdate.

How do I get a copy of the StocksUpdate?

The StocksUpdate is a benefit of being a member of the Truly Rich Club. The Truly Rich Club is an online group created by Bo Sanchez. It's called "Truly Rich" because the members are taught not only to be financially wealthy, but also how to be blessed in the areas of life: relationships, career, spirituality, health, and of course finances.

Bo believed that being rich is useless if you're not healthy, or if you don't have the energy to enjoy your money. Having a lot of money will also be useless if you don't have people to enjoy it with!

That's why he takes on a very holistic and practical approach to achieving financial abundance in the Truly Rich Club.

As a member, you get e-books, recordings of live seminars, and financial newsletters aside from the StocksUpdate. Now, I'll just give a quick run through of the things you'll get as a Truly Rich Club member because I believe that this is the best guidance you can get as you start investing.

The Truly Rich Club Member Benefits

In the following table, I've outlined what you'll get as a member, including the StocksUpdate.

Benefit

1. **StocksUpdate:** Your ultimate step-by-step guide to investing in the stock market (as shown in the previous sections).

2. **Power Talks:** These are the best of Bo's seminar recordings every month. These are inspirational and transformative talks that will teach you how to live the life that want. (Sent twice a month)

3. **Success Mentors Collection:** These are interview recordings of Bo with his mentor's like Edward Lee (stock market), Larry Gamboa (real estate), and many others. Through these interviews, you get to learn not only from Bo,

but other experts as well. (Sent quarterly)

4. **Wealth Strategies:** This is a newsletter that gives you financial education. Topics range from the principles of abundance to the nitty-gritty details of business, insurance and other investments.

Bonus: Free Learning Materials!

These are the one-time bonuses that you'll

receive when you sign-up:

- Audio: How to be Truly Rich Seminar

- E-book: How to Turn Thoughts into Things

- E-book: How to Conquer Your Goliaths

Bonus: Earn Online as an Affiliate

As a member of the Truly Rich Club, you're also given the opportunity to earn online. If you share the Truly Rich Club with friends and family (and they sign-up) using your link, you will get to earn a commission. This is just to give the members a taste of "passive income".

*Please take note that this is only a bonus and it's purely optional.

100% Transparency Disclaimer: Since I am a member of the Truly Rich Club, I have the bonus opportunity to earn some income from it. So when you sign up using my link, I will get a commission from your subscription. However, income aside, my recommendation is always based on my personal experience that the product provides excellent and valuable service.

Stock Market for Pinoys Affiliate Bonus: Now, since I'll be earning a small amount of money when you join the Truly Rich Club using my link (visit www.StockMarketforPinoys.com/trc/begin), I'd like to give you additional bonuses when you sign-up, just as a thank you.

The Membership Cost

Membership to the Truly Rich Club is not free. I am currently paying P497 per month (roughly P17/day) to get these benefits. There are also other membership options which have different prices and benefits. The details need not be discussed here. However, what I think you'll find interesting is that there's a "30-day 'no-questions-asked' money back guarantee". This means you can try out the membership, get 100% access to the materials, and then if you don't like it, just ask for a refund. They will give your money back, with no questions asked. So, there's absolutely no risk to just try it out.

Interesting… So it's okay that I just follow the Truly Rich Club list?

You have to read this section first. You see, the only time following a stock recommendation list would be irresponsible is if you act on it blindly, without knowing the source and its credibility. Let me explain using this story:

There was a young and beautiful girl, who lived in a hut by the ocean, named Marimar. Her evil aunt, named Angelica, told Marimar that her husband Sergio has been cheating on her.

Being very gullible, Marimar believed Angelica and went home crying to seek comfort from her dog, Polgoso. Marimar was so angry and hopeless (and irresponsible) that she packed her things and left the country without saying goodbye to anyone. During the trip, she got into an accident and died.

Now, Marimar failed to do something that she should have done after she got the information. She should have first checked the credibility of two things: the credibility of the source of information and the credibility of the information itself.

(For the benefit of the very young readers, the above story is just a reference to the 1994 Telenovela entitled Marimar. It was a show that swept the Philippine TV during its time. I still have the introductory song memorized! Oh, and the story above wasn't the real plot of the show.)

Anyway, whenever you're following a stock recommendation list, it is a must to know the credibility of the source and the reliability of the information. You need to ask:

- Who is the person making the recommendation? (Source Credibility)

- How well have these recommendations been performing?

(Information Credibility)

Truly Rich Club Credibility

The founder of the Truly Rich Club is Bo Sanchez. He is a spiritual preacher, best-selling author, publisher, international speaker, entrepreneur, millionaire, philanthropist, father, and husband. He has built many ministries for the poor and less fortunate; he has achieved many awards, and the list of his accomplishments is just too many to mention here.

Now, I'd like to make something clear here: Bo Sanchez is not a stock market expert. If he were the one doing the analysis, I wouldn't be so comfortable following the recommendations. However, I'm a strong believer in the Truly Rich Club recommendations because of Bo's mentor and partner in the stock market, Edward Lee.

Edward Lee is known as the "Warren Buffet" of the Philippines. He is a self-made billionaire and the chairman and founder of CitisecOnline. He started investing in the stock market when he was only 18 years old. Today, he has almost 40 years of experience under his belt. It is because of Edward Lee that the credibility of the Truly Rich Club is unrivaled.

Under the guidance of Edward Lee, the Truly Rich Club has been recommending stocks for the past two years. And so far, the performance has been stellar.

I encourage you to join the Truly Rich Club as you start investing in the stock market. It's the best guidance out there, and you get a complete package for your financial education.

Take the Leap - Quick Tip!

Join the Truly Rich Club. With the StocksUpdate newsletter, it would be like having an expert babysitter for your investing. You'll know exactly: (1) What companies to buy, (2) When exactly to buy them, (3) At what prices to buy them, and (4) When to sell them.

Important: When you sign up, remember to sign up through any of the links in this book, or on the stockmarketforpinoys.com website. That way, I'll be able to give you exclusive bonuses and step-by-step tutorials on how to invest the Truly Rich Club Way.

Truly Rich Club Links

1. Signing up and Getting the Stock Market for Pinoys.com Bonuses

2. Truly Rich Club More Information Page

3. Performance Review of the Stocks Update Recommendations

4. Video Tour of the Truly Rich Club

SECTION 2: STOCK MARKET EXPLORING TO THE FULLEST

This part is purely optional. However, it is suggested that you still read it. I've only included this part for people who are more curious than the rest. So, there are many investors who have no clue about the topics listed below, and it doesn't hurt them (even if they don't know it). But of course, the more you know, the better, right?

On Initial Public Offerings (IPO)

What is an IPO?

An IPO is short for 'Initial Public Offering.' This refers to the first time the public is given an opportunity to buy shares of a new, publicly-listed company. Of course, this happens after PSE screens the company to protect the investing public.

IPOs are very exciting since they may present an opportunity to make a lot of money. The investing public is a bit biased towards IPOs. People remember, retell, and exaggerate the money they made on the successful ones, while the IPOs that failed or performed less than spectacular are quickly forgotten or castigated (you may have read a lot of stories about Facebook's IPO on the internet).

Here are three IPO examples and their stories:

PureGold's opening day was a bad day. Its opening price was P12.50, but it closed at P11.00. If you sold your shares immediately on that day, you would have already lost 12% of your money. However, for those who stuck with it for the next couple of months, they would have nearly doubled their money.

East West Bank's IPO opening day seemed like a good start since its price shot up to P19.78 from P18.50. However, you'll see that the excitement quickly died down in the following days.

The IPO of **Cebu Pacific** was also well received on its opening day. News also said that it was "oversubscribed." This meant that a lot of people wanted to buy the stock. It climbed from P125 to P133 on its first day. However, after several months, the stock price gradually declined. Many people held on to the stock believing that it would one day get back up again. One year passed, but sadly the stock price dropped even more. (In July 2012, the stock price was only in the P67 - P70 range.

How do I get into an IPO?

The first person to go to if you want to get into an IPO is your stockbroker. If you have an online broker and don't see any notifications on your home screen, then it would be best to call them.

As soon as you hear the news of an IPO, contact them to ask when you can get the shares. Do not wait until the opening date since that would already be too late.

In an IPO, the shares of stock are limited to each person. This means you can't "hoard" the shares (but there are probably people who work around this). For instance, in the PureGold IPO, the limit was at 1,000 shares per account only.

Is getting into an IPO advisable?

Investing in an IPO entails a lot of risk since the company is usually still new and not all of the information about the company has been 'absorbed' by the public. Add to that the emotional rush it creates - the excitement from everybody wanting to get it and the fear from missing out on an opportunity. This emotional rush makes a lot of investors blind to the risk of not knowing anything about the company.

Imagine this scenario:

Ellie just heard about the IPO of Abakada Company. Ellie is a cautious and patient investor, so she waits for more information before getting into it. Ellie then receives a text from her friend asking, "Will you be buying Abakada IPO?"

Ellie says that she's still thinking about. The friend taunts her, "Don't wait anymore; you should get into it! It's a really good company."

While browsing on Facebook, Ellie sees a post: "Just got in Abakada IPO, woohoo!" She looks at who the post is from, but doesn't recognize the person. It must be one of the random people she added just to get the notifications down to zero.

Later that evening, Ellie went to her Tita's birthday party. While having dinner, she overheard one of the tables talking about investing. It was the "Chinese-Tito's" table.

Since the table was already full, she just tried to listen to their conversation. After a few minutes of listening, she learns that several of them already signed up for the IPO.

The next morning, Ellie calls up her broker and also asks to get her shares for the coming IPO.

Did Ellie learn anything about the company? Not a thing.

What she did find out was that a lot of other people were also getting into it. And that shouldn't be enough reason to justify investing in any company.

I'm very familiar with this scenario since it has happened to me. I got the texts. I saw the posts on Facebook. Instead of a birthday party, it was a Despedida. Instead of the Chinese-tito table, it was my sister's high school friends table. And the moment I signed up for the stocks, I also encouraged my other friends to get into it. Fortunately, I didn't end up losing money.

One of the most lethal get-rich-quick toxins that poisoned the mind of the investing public in the 1990s was the idea you could build wealth by buying IPOs. Investing in an IPO sounds like a great idea – after all, if you had bought 100 shares of Microsoft when it went public in 1986, your $2,100 investment would have grown to $720,000 by early 2003.

Unfortunately, for every IPO like Microsoft that turns out to be a big winner, there are a thousand losers. Psychologists Kahneman and Tversky have shown when humans estimate the likelihood of an event, we make that judgment based not on how often the event has occurred, but on how vivid the past examples are.

We all want to buy "the next Microsoft" – precisely because we know we missed buying the first Microsoft. But we conveniently overlook the fact that most other IPOs were terrible investments.

-from the commentary by Jason Zweig of "The Intelligent Investor" by Benjamin Graham

BASIC STOCK MARKET TERMS

In this section, I'll quickly provide the meaning of basic stock market terms. You'll encounter them as soon as you create your account with an online broker. There will be a bit of technical and boring stuff here, but don't worry about not understanding it at the moment. This is because in part 3 of this e-book, I've provided you with links to step-by-step video and text tutorials on how to go about these items. So, for now, it's enough that you just read through this once to get acquainted with the terms. You'll understand these concepts more when you get started.

Stock Symbol or Stock Code

In the stock market, each company is assigned a nickname (or a code). This is called the stock symbol. You don't need to memorize all of them, since you'll be provided with a 'cheat sheet' when you're making a transaction.

Market Price

The market price is simply the price per share of a particular stock. When the stock market is open, the price can change every second. It all depends on how much the buyers want to buy, and how much the sellers want to sell.

Bid and Ask Price / Size

You will see the bid and ask price when you want to place an order. You will probably see something that looks like a table. To understand this table of bidding and asking prices, you need to remember that for a transaction to happen, buyers and sellers must "agree" on the price. Naturally, buyers would want to buy at the lowest price possible, while sellers would want to sell at the highest price possible.

This bid/ask table just shows the buyers and sellers meeting point. This is why this table shows the highest buying prices and the lowest selling prices.

Tick Size

The fluctuation or tick size is the smallest increment in the price of a stock. These tick sizes vary depending on the price range that stock belongs to.

If there were no tick sizes, buyers and sellers have an infinite range of prices to bid and sell. This would make it more difficult to facilitate the trades.

Lot Size

Board Lots are also standard increments set by the PSE, but this time the minimum allowable increment affects the number of shares to be bought or sold.

Board Lot

The board lot is simply a table showing the summary of the tick sizes and the lot sizes of the respective price ranges of the stocks.

Limit Orders vs. Market Orders

When you buy or sell using a market order, you pay or receive the current going rate for a stock. Limit orders allow you to set a limit. For example, you can set a highest price you're willing to pay per share and only deal with those willing to sell at that price. This gives you a bit more control - and ensures you get the best deals available.

Whoa! That was a LOT of Technical Information!

Yes, sorry for that! I hope your nose didn't bleed. But don't worry, because you don't have to understand it all at this time. You'll understand it better when you have an account and are going through the actual buying and selling of stocks.

So the technical information you saw up there - we'll go through it in depth with the other step-by-step guides you'll be able to access in Part 3 of this guide. I've made those step-by-step guides in such a way that even a grade school student will be able to follow it – it is a 110% spoon feeding guide. So with that, read on!

ON MORE LEARNING

In this section, you will find my recommended references for further study. I have arranged it in increasing order of complexity (the further down the list, the harder it is to read). So my suggestion is to start doing them from the top of the list per category.

Included in these references are books, e-books, websites, and seminars you can look at to further your learning in those topics. Most of the books listed here at available at National, Power Books or Fully Booked. For the other references, links are provided for more information.

Now, take note that you already know enough to start investing in the stock market. Reading these references below would be good, but it isn't necessary for you to get started. You can do it at the same time you begin investing.

ABUNDANCE MINDSET

<u>"How to Be Truly Rich" Seminar by Bo Sanchez</u>

– Ninety percent of money problems are problems of the mind. In this seminar, Bo Sanchez teaches you how to enlarge your "psychological wallet," and prepare your mind to receive abundant blessings. If you join the Truly Rich Club, you already get the recording. (More Information Here)

"Truly Rich Club" Membership by Bo Sanchez – In the Truly Rich Club, you get an overflow of blessings with e-books, audio tapes, seminar recordings, and wealth articles that will guide you in your journey to becoming Truly Rich. In this club, you'll be taught how to be truly rich in all areas of your life: finances, relationships, career, spirituality, and health. (More Information Here)

***The Millionaire Next Door* by Stanley Ph.D. and Danko PhD** – In this book, you'll learn about the wealth habits of the millionaires in America. After reading this, you'll be a lot more conscious of the things that make you richer and the things that make you poorer.

ON INVESTING

***Rich Dad, Poor Dad* by Robert Kiyosaki** – This is the best book that can explain, in very simple terms, how to become rich. It teaches about the difference of real assets and real liabilities. Knowledge of this basic principle will change how you decide what to invest in.

***Who Took My Money* by Robert Kiyosaki** – This book teaches about becoming a more patient investor. Its basic principle is that those who are patient in learning get the highest returns while those who are impatient (want to get the easiest form of investments) get the worst kinds of returns.

__The Intelligent Investor__ **by Benjamin Graham** – This is a classic when it comes to the world of investing. It teaches "value investing"- a set of principles which guides investors how to become more discerning.

STOCK MARKET: LONG TERM INVESTMENT:

__The Turtle Always Wins__ **by Bo Sanchez** – This is a sequel to "My Maid Invests in the Stock Market." It explains the four kinds of investors in the stock market. It also shows how and why investing for the long term beats the short term traders.

__Buffetology__ **by Mary Buffet** – Warren Buffet is the world's greatest investor. In this book, you'll learn about his techniques, which have allowed him to get the greatest returns over long periods.

__Warren Buffet and the Interpretation of Financial Statements__ – This book provides simple explanations of how to understand financial statements. It's a must-read for those who want to take fundamental analysis seriously.

MARKET TIMING, TRADING / TECHNICAL ANALYSIS

COL Technical Analysis Seminars – This is a two-part seminar held once a month by CitisecOnline.

Registration is free for current CitisecOnline members. (More Information and Registration Here)

www.Swing–Trade-Stocks.com – This website contains a very structured tutorial on how to time the market. Articles are appropriately separated into beginner, intermediate, and advanced topics.

Other Seminars – I haven't attended all of the seminars available regarding technical analysis. But as a quick guideline here, only attend a technical analysis seminar if that is the ONLY topic for the WHOLE day. Do not attend seminars wherein you'll be taught the basics plus technical analysis, or technical plus fundamental analysis. Technical analysis is a course which is good for a minimum of 8 hours - and that's with a good teacher. That's why the seminar you want to attend should purely be focused on technical analysis alone, for the whole day.

Beating the Market

To start, let me introduce you to Warren Buffett. Mr. Buffett has been the single most successful investor since the late 1950's. Let's set the stage. The year is 1984. Recently, there had arisen a growing consensus that the stock market was fully efficient, called "Efficient Market Theory." Academics and investors were declaring it impossible for someone to consistently pick stocks that would beat the overall market average because everything was priced in already. Columbia Business School hosted an epic debate as a contest between Michael Jensen, a professor from the University of Rochester and one of the leading voices of the Efficient Market Theory, versus Warren Buffett, famed stock-picker. Jensen went first. He argued that if you flipped a coin 50 times, there would be someone that happened to get heads 50 times in a row, but that didn't mean that that person had skill. He called picking stocks a "coin flip."

Ten Buffett spoke. He said "let's imagine that we had a coin-flipping contest. And that, of course, we could have some lucky winners and losers. But then, let's assume that all the winners had something in common.

What if all the winners of the coin-flipping contest came from Omaha, or had an unusual technique? Wouldn't you be curious to find out what made this high concentration of winners? Buffett then went through the investment performance of nine successful investors that just so happened to all practice the same methodology and all had the same teachers, Benjamin Graham and David Dodd. He called them "The Super-Investors of Graham-and-Doddsville." Buffett was unequivocally declared the winner after his masterful speech. No one could doubt the numbers or the logic. The clear conclusion is that you can be successful in picking stocks; and it requires following the investment principles of Graham, Dodd, and Buffett.

Buffett references Benjamin Graham and David L. Dodd. Together, Graham and Dodd wrote *Security*

Analysis in 1934. This book, still in print after several editions, has influenced many great investors since the very first YOUNG INVESTORS SOCIETY. Additionally, Benjamin Graham wrote *The Intelligent Investor* in 1949. Mr. Buffett first read this book in 1950 and considers it, "by far the best book on investing ever written." Benjamin Graham is considered the father of value investing, and so we start here. As you read the article make a note of the key concepts that are referenced. Some are repeated several times.

Questions to Consider:

1. What are the common traits of successful investors?

2. If there is a clear recipe for investment success, why do you think so few people follow it?

The Seven Golden Rules

Like any venture, a set of rules can offer guidance in your investments that can lead to greater success. This is one set of rules developed by investing geniuses.

When you are successful in investing in the stock market, you make money. Sometimes a great deal of money. One of the biggest names in the investment world, and one we have studied above, is Warren Buffett. He started by investing $10,000 - and he turned that into a net worth of $60 BILLION!! And he's not the only one. There are many others who have made their fortune in the stock market. You may not have $10,000 in cash to spare. But you can certainly use what you do have to enrich your own net worth.

Rule 1: Think Long-Term

You are unlikely to make millions overnight, or even in the first year or two of investment. You have to look beyond a company's short-term downfalls and into the potential for future growth. For example, American Express stocks took a major hit in 1964. This is when Warren Buffett stepped in and scooped it up. A decade into the future, he didn't regret it.

Rule 2: Good Companies Make Good Investments

Investing in the stock market isn't about having a crystal ball or trying to get ahold of market information a moment before the next person. You can't predict which stocks will grow and when. But, you can identify good companies with solid business plans and invest your money in stocks worthy of it.

- Good Companies:
  o have a unique advantage that isn't easily replicated by competitors.
  o Generate high returns on capital.
  o Don't borrow much money, because their business finances itself.

Rule 3: Buy with a Safety Margin

One of the most-read books by professional investors is Benjamin Graham's *The Intelligent Investor*.

This is where the concept of the "Margin of Safety" was introduced. The idea here is that if you buy a business at a low enough price that if you're wrong, your loss would not be significant.

Rule 4: Do Your Own Homework and Know What You Own

You can't take the advice of anyone who comes along when it comes to your investments. You have to know your portfolio and understand the companies you are a part owner in.

Rule 5: Don't Follow the Herd: Stay Calm and Rational

Many investors make the same mistakes - buying when others are buying, and selling when others are selling. This is a strategy that will get you the results of the many. And you're looking to experience the results of the few. Keeping calm is the best way to avoid this downfall.

Rule 6: Don't Put All Your Eggs in One Basket - But Don't have Too Many Baskets, Either

Remember the power of diversification. Having a well-rounded portfolio reduces your risk of taking an overall loss on your investment. But keep in mind the wisdom of studying just a few companies, gaining intimate knowledge of them.

Diversification protects your portfolio from market setbacks. For example, if your entire investment is held up in one corporation that sells beef and the company is plagued by an outbreak of E. coli, you could see a rapid downturn, even possibly a 100% loss! Diversifying helps you balance out the risks of multiple stocks so that one company's loss doesn't in turn lose your entire retirement savings.

One way to diversify investments is to make use of a mutual fund, which holds a basket of investments in a variety of corporations. Using the knowledge base of experts in diversification can earn you a feeling of greater security, though you sacrifice the benefits of being your own broker that we mentioned earlier.

Research shows that 90% of the benefits of diversification can be obtained with a portfolio of just over 20 stocks. Once you diversify further, you begin to have less knowledge and understanding of the companies you're working with.

Diversify, but remember you want to invest only in those companies you believe in, rather than building a varied portfolio of companies you're not so sure about.

Rule 7: Never Stop Learning

This is probably the most important rule - in stock market investing as well as in life. You can never learn too much about topics that interest you. Even the greatest investors take the opportunity to learn from one another. Warren Buffett credits much of his success to other investors such as Charlie Munger and Benjamin Graham.

BONUS: Find Meaningful Ways to Give Back

Often we hear more about the most wealthy among us because of their efforts at giving back to the community than we hear about their financial successes. Bill and Melinda Gates have dedicated much of their fortune to battling poverty and improving the quality of education across the nation and throughout the world. Warren Buffett has committed his billions to improving life for others around him, rather than simply padding his own bank account. You don't have to make billions to give back. You can commit a percentage of your earnings to a charity of your choice. Or simply use some of the time your healthier financial situation has lent you to donate your time to those in need.

SECTION 3 : STOCK MARKET VALUES!

Imagine in front of you is a box containing a dozen doughnuts. How much would you pay for one donut? If all the donuts in the box are the same, is one worth more than the other? What if the world had a shortage of sugar and this was the last box of donuts in the world, with none being able to be made for the next year, does the scarcity increase the value of the good? How about if you just ate a box of donuts and can't eat anymore, does the value you would pay for a donut decrease?

The box of 12 doughnuts represents a company. When you break the company down, everyone has an opportunity to own some of the donuts, or part of the company. But people may pay wildly different prices for the same donut. If you want to maximize the value of a box of donuts, what might be the best approach? One method is to convince people that these are the tastiest donuts in the world and they will only be around for a limited time. In a nutshell, this is how the market works. The stock market is made up of people who get excited about something or sick of something depending on their mood. What is obvious is that occasionally the market goes nuts!

What Is The Value Of A Business?

We'll only invest in a company when the price we

pay today is significantly less than the value we will get tomorrow.

Example: A teacher picks a student at random. The teacher holds up a $10 bill and asks the student, "What is the value of this bill?" Ten dollars. The teacher holds up ten $1 bills. She asks the same question, "What is the value of these dollar bills?" Ten dollars. The teacher offers to sell the student the $10 bill for the ten 1 dollar bills. This is a wash, so maybe he'll take it, maybe he won't.

Then the Teacher offers to sell the $10 for only five 1 dollar bills. Of course, he should take it. Ask the question to the rest of the class at large, "How many of you would buy this?" Do the reverse. Ask to sell the $10 bill for twenty $1 bills? How many would take this? None of them.

The best investors can snatch up $10 bills when the market is only asking $5 for them. But how is this possible? It is possible because a. the value is tricky to calculate, and b. the market is irrational.

Remember the Market goes nuts. Is this a good thing or a bad thing for you? It's a very good thing. If all investors based their investment decisions on rational and conservative estimates of intrinsic value, it would be very difficult to make money in the stock market. Fortunately, the participants in the stock market are humans subject to the corroding influence of emotions.

Many investors will give into the hype around

stocks, or people will hop on a trend because they have optimistic views that they can beat the system. As young investment geniuses, we will always check emotions at the door and buy stocks based on what they are worth.

Understanding the Terminology

A company's worth – which is its total value – is called its market capitalization and it is represented by the company's stock price. Market cap (as it is commonly referred to) is equal to the stock price multiplied by the number of shares outstanding.

For example, a stock with a $5 stock price and 10 million shares outstanding/trading is worth $50 million ($5 x 10 million). If we take this one step further, we can see that a company that has a $10 stock price and one million shares outstanding (market cap = $10 million) is worth less than a company with a $5 stock price and 10 million shares outstanding (market cap = $50 million).

Thus, the stock price is a relative and proportional value of a company's worth and only represents percentage changes in market cap at any given point in time. Any percentage changes in a stock price will result in an equal percentage change in a company's value. This is the reason investors are so concerned with stock prices and any changes that may occur since even a $0.10 drop in a $5 stock can result in a $100,000 loss for shareholders with one million shares.

Questions To Consider:

1. What is the Market Cap of a Company with a stock price of $20/share and 10 million shares outstanding?

2. What is the current Market Cap of Apple? How many shares do they have outstanding and what is the stock price?

The next logical question is: Who sets stock prices and how are they calculated? In simple terms, the stock price of a company is calculated when a company goes on sale to the public; an event called an initial public offering.

This is when a company will pay an investment bank a lot of money to use very complex formulas and valuation techniques to derive a company's value by determining how many shares will be offered to the public and at what price. For example, a company whose value is estimated at $100 million may want to issue 10 million shares at $10 per share, or they may want to issue 20 million at $5 a share.

As we saw in the example with Apple, a company's value is dependent on how much the company can grow its earnings in the future. When a company sells more items or enters a new market or improves margins, it can grow profits.

The "Go-To" Way to Value a Business: P/E Ratio

One way to determine the value of a business is with the Price-to-Earnings Ratio or P/E Ratio.

The price-earnings ratio can be calculated as:

Market Value per Share (Stock Price) / Earnings per Share

For example, suppose that a company is currently trading at $43 a share and its earnings over the last 12 months were $1.95 per share. The P/E ratio for the stock could then be calculated as $43/$1.95, or about 22x.

In essence, the price-earnings ratio indicates how many years an investor has to wait at the current earnings to get all their money back. If the P/E ratio is 22x, you are saying at this level of earnings; it will take you 22 years for the company to earn how much you bought the stock for $43. In general, a high P/E suggests that investors are expecting higher earnings growth in the future compared to companies with a lower P/E. A low P/E can indicate either a company may currently be undervalued or the company's profits are expected to decline.

Think of a P/E as the price you pay for a stock.

In general, there are a couple of Price / Earnings (P/E) rules of thumb:

The average P/E over the past decade is 15. An average company, should be worth about 15.

Really great companies (very high returns with consistent earnings growth) tend to trade about 20-25x P/E.

Bad companies, ones whose earnings are unpredictable and make low returns, usually trade at below 10x P/E.

A company should trade at about the P/E as its earnings are expected to grow in the future. Companies growing profits 30% per year may be justified to trade at 30x P/E. Companies growing 15% per year may trade at 15x P/E. Companies not growing may trade at 5-10x P/E.

As you can see, valuing stocks is like going to a grocery store. You get what you pay for. If you want to buy the best product, you're likely going to have to pay for it.

There are two reasons to buy companies with a low P/E ratio:

- The company may be undervalued.

- The company most likely has high earnings.

Key Takeaways

1. Stocks fluctuate wildly on a yearly basis. The true value of the business does not actually change much.

2. If someone offers you a dollar for fifty cents, take it!

3. The two most important things that determine the value of a company are: a. how much profits are going to grow to, and b. how long that profit

level is sustainable.

4. The P/E ratio is a good starting point to determine the value of a company.

What Makes A Good Business?

Think finding a good long-term business is easy? Just take a quick look at history, and you'll see that only a handful of companies survive over time. For example, create a list of businesses that have failed or gone bankrupt in the past 20 years. (Examples: Chrysler, Enron, Delta Airlines, Countrywide Mortgages, and Lehman Brothers) Why do you think that some companies succeed while others fail? How can we identify the winners from the losers for investment purposes?

How do I Know if a Company is a Good Business?

Economic Moats

When we think of moats, we may envision the body of water surrounding a castle or fortress. The economic moat is essentially the same. It is a type of protection a company holds from external forces. There are many types, and each are excellent indicators that a company is a great place to invest your money. Below are the different types of moats:

- **Intangible Assets:** Brands, patents, and regulatory licenses may allow a company to sell products or services that can't be replicated by competitors.

- **High Switching Costs:** Products and services offered to consumers on a contract can make it difficult for those consumers to switch to another company, providing some power in pricing and additional economic security.

- **Network Effect:** Some companies benefit from network economics, one of the most powerful moats. The network effect means that the more consumers are in the network, the better the value they find in the product or service. It is mutually beneficial to both the company and the consumer, which also creates a strong sense of loyalty.

- **Low-Cost Advantage:** Some companies experience certain advantages that cause them to be able to offer their goods and services at a cost much lower than competing companies, which offers a lasting economic moat.

Learning Check:

1. What is a company that comes to mind when you think of those with a wide and powerful moat? What company is likely to stand strong 10 years from now.

2. What is a company with a narrow moat? What company is currently doing well, but you don't see standing the test of time.

3. Now, what about a company in which you can't identify any moat at all? What company is just a

bad business both now and in the future.

Quick Matching Game:

The following companies have stood the test of time, which probably indicates they have some sort of economic moat. Can you identify what their economic moat is? (intangible assets, high switching costs, network effect, low cost advantage)

- Coca Cola

- Bank of America

- Google

- Wal-Mart

- Exxon Mobil

Hint: There can be more than one per company!

Conclusion

All businesses are not created equal: some are bad, most are average, but some are really, really good. Selling candy is better than selling rats, and even better is selling Coca-Cola or iPhones. The goal of the long term investor is to identify really good companies that can earn high returns on capital for decades into the future. The only way to defend these high returns though is with a deep economic moat.

The surest way to make money in the stock market is to invest in good companies that make exceptional returns and can defend these returns for decades into the future. In this lesson, you have learned how to identify these companies. If you master this skill, you will gain one of the most valuable investing tools a great investor will ever learn.

Key Takeaways:

❖ Most businesses will fail.

❖ There are some exceptional businesses out there that have an "economic moat".

❖ Great companies have the economic moats of Intangible Assets / Brands, High Switching Costs, Network Effects or a Low Cost Advantage.

❖ Don't open a rat store.

Warren Buffett

"Time is the friend of the wonderful company, the enemy of the mediocre."

SECTION 4: LEAP!

Now that you already know everything you need to begin investing in the stock market, I'll be showing you the specific steps you should take to get started. In this section, please note that my focus is the action step itself, so I will no longer elaborate on ideas which have been discussed in part 1 and part 2 of this guide.

I will only give specific instructions which will move you further along your journey in investing.

My goal here is to get you started with your investments in the fastest and most effective way possible.

So bear in mind that rather than present you with Options A, B and C, I will just instruct you to do X, Y and then Z.

Day 1: Commit to a Personal Investing Goal

The first thing that you will need to get started is your commitment. While that's such a cliché statement, it needs to be said – and repeated. Nothing will happen without your commitment.

Right now, it doesn't matter if you're rich or poor, a college graduate or a drop-out, an employee or an entrepreneur. It doesn't matter where you're coming from – all that matters is where you're going. So at this moment, the only thing that matters is if you're willing to improve your financial life and start investing in the stock market.

With that said, I'd like you to commit to a goal that you will be moving toward financial freedom. It could be about investing for yourself, or for the people you love. The important thing here is that you decide and commit to it.

Creating Your Personal Investing Goal!

First, write down your *WHY!* The most important thing is to know why you're investing. Are you investing so that you can enjoy a carefree retirement? Are you hoping to retire early? Do you want to send your children to college debt-free? Purchase a home in cash? Leave behind a legacy for your family? This is what you will need to keep in mind throughout your investing adventure.

Write down your personal investing goal and put it where you'll see it frequently. This way, every time you see it, you'll be reminded of the promise you have made to yourself. Commit to yourself. Know that you are worth the effort. You are worth the risk. And your outcomes are within your control.

Here is a sample of a goal you might write. You'll notice it contains the investment goal, which is cut and dry (10% or more of salary). If you simply commit to investing in general without an amount in mind, setting aside the funds for investment will not maintain the level of priority it requires. You'll also notice that written within the goal is the WHY. Without remembering why we are making a choice, again, the level of priority will downshift. Your plans for investment in the stock market will be much like your last New Year's Resolution - likely forgotten within the first month.

I am consistently investing 10% or more of my salary so that I can comfortably retire and spend more time with the people I love and care about.

Day 2: Create an Account with CitisecOnline or your broker of choice.

Now, it's time to move forward and create an account with CitisecOnline (or the broker you choose). We have listed online brokers in another section of this book. Each have their advantages and disadvantages. Make sure to do your homework. You can find comparison charts online listing the features, fees, and what traders love or hate about working with them.

It may take 2-3 days for COLFinancial (or the online broker of your choice) to process your forms from the time they receive them. So it's really good if you start as soon as possible. One of my friends told me that she didn't act on this very quickly when she was starting. She was already excited to get started, but for some reason, she only filled out the forms and never sent them to COLFinancial. Then, without her knowing, several months passed by with her forms accumulating dust in the drawer. Now, I hope you don't let this happen to you. So act now, act now, and act now.

Check in daily and have the funds available and ready to invest. Be excited and count down the days until your account is active and you are ready to trade! Have your plan in place. Know what you're planning to buy and what you're willing to pay. Practice tracking the stocks while you wait and build the anticipation. This is an exciting new journey you're about to begin!

Day 3: Try Out or Sign-up To the Truly Rich Club (Or Another Service)

In my opinion, Truly Rich Club is the best guide out there for beginners and even veterans. You have worked hard for your money, and I think your money deserves the best "babysitter" (Edward Lee) out there. Ultimately, what this can mean for you is not only profitability, but peace of mind. To know that you're being guided by the best means you can sleep soundly while your money works hard for you.

Now, I think of the Truly Rich Club as being able to hire the best stock market expert here in the Philippines (Edward Lee) so that he can tell me exactly what to buy and sell.

There are many similar services available online. Again, you'll want to do your homework to determine which is the best fit for you and your needs. There are U.S. based agencies as well. Different investment experts have different approaches. Take a peak at a few different ones and see who aligns best with your goals and priorities.

However, if paying for expert guidance is not your thing, another other option is to look at the COL EIP recommendation list. As of Nov 2012, they are recommending 16 different companies that you can invest in for the long term. Now, please take note here that with this COL EIP list, you will be on your own. So it's important that you have the discipline and confidence to keep on investing in your selected companies.

If you can't decide at the moment, then just go for the Truly Rich Club and try it out. There's a 30-day money back guarantee anyway. So you can just "see what it's like" first.

Day 4: Buy your First Stock

From your list from the TRC or EIP, pick out a company that you like and buy it. Two to three companies from different industries would be a good enough diversification at this point. Start out small and consistently make additional purchases to build your portfolio as you get the hang of it. You'll learn as you go. You'll also build confidence along the way that will help guide your activities.

Day 5: Monitor Your Investment

Congratulations!

You are invested in the stock market.

Feel free to watch your investments go green (up), and go red (down). The important thing to remind yourself here is that you are a long-term investor and that these small price movements don't matter.

Right now, you should be proud that business tycoons are working hard to make your money grow. (Recall that if you buy a stock, you are buying into a business, and you are leveraging on the people running that business.) While those working for the company are hard at work, your money is doing your work for you.

Day 6: Stick to Your Investing Strategy

Next month or next quarter, make sure to invest your savings into the stock market. Remember that your original investment grows if you don't keep on planting. It doesn't matter how small you put in every month; the important thing is that you are accumulating wealth.

Now, as you begin to invest in the stock market, you will notice that a lot of people will be boasting about their investing strategies. You will hear about people making 50+% over the past month, and it's natural to get a little envious of this.

But it is at this point that you need to stick to your strategy because of the following reasons:

1. You do not know how much money these people have lost in the past. Most probably they are only sharing their wins.

2. You do not know how long these people study

the stock market, and how exactly they study it. They may be spending several hours a day so they can execute their trades.

3. You do not know what kind of rules they follow with their trades.

4. You do not know when they bought that stock or when they sold it.

If you want to venture into a new strategy, you need to preserve your current strategy, and just set aside a portion for this adventure. For example, if you're investing $2000 monthly, you can divide that amount into two portions: The first portion is for your slow but sure way of investing, and the other portion is for the new strategy. In this manner, you secure your core long-term investment, while you get to explore other strategies.

Day 7: Share the Knowledge

This isn't surprising, considering we were never taught how to invest. Our teachers didn't teach us, nor did our parents. After all, how could they teach us if no one taught them, either?

I am saying this to you so that you can appreciate the person who introduced you to the stock market and made you download this book. Thank that person, because the knowledge that you gained here is so very rare.

I sincerely hope that since you're almost done

reading this book, you will be investing in the Stock Market within the week (or at most within the month). And when you finally get to start investing in the stock market, hopefully you can share the knowledge here.

This way, sometime in the future, the majority of working-class individuals will have the much-deserved convenience of making their money work hard for them. Let's end the poverty. Let's spread financial literacy. It is one thing to learn how to invest and grow your wealth. As with anything, we know we have truly learned, on the highest level, when we are able to teach others.

The BONUS step we discussed earlier was the importance of giving back once you've made your fortune. One sure way to give back is to help others create wealth through investing in the stock market.

Investing in Your Future

As you continue your journey into investing in the stock market, keep in mind the discussion we had in the first section of this book about your financial future. Upon retirement, will you have 30+ years of expenses available to you? Or will you be living a life filled with stress and uncertainty? Will you be enjoying a much-earned life of leisure, traveling and spending quality time with family and friends? Or will you be working full time long into your golden years, until you've reached a point of exhaustion that doesn't allow for fulfilling the lifelong dreams you had always assumed you would have time for later on?

For the vast majority of working-class individuals, Social Security benefits and the retirement plan offered by our employers are simply not enough to sustain comfortable lifestyles. Yet if we start now, putting our money to work for us, we could be in a much better financial situation, potentially even able to leave behind a legacy for our beloved family members.

Remember – if you are currently in debt, eliminating your debt is your first priority. Money owed creates more money owed and paying interest and fees on your debt will counteract any good you're doing yourself in investments. Handle the debt first – and invest only the money you won't need in the near future.

Initial investments can be small. You may consider adding to your portfolio in small, frequent amounts. You may not miss just $50 per month that you commit to investing. But over time, even small sums add up, especially when given time to grow. Watching your money grow will give you the confidence and the added motivation to begin investing more. You may find ways to cut back on spending so that you have more available to invest. And all investments made work for you toward the goals you've set for yourself and your future.

Advice from Investment Experts

Let's hear from some of the many men and women who have made millions (even billions) investing in the stock market.

"Investors should purchase stocks like they purchase groceries, not like they purchase perfume"

Ben Graham

One can find two distinct interpretations here.

- You MUST prioritize your investment goals as you would those chores most important to you.

- Keep in mind the companies that are most secure are those offering the essentials - grocery markets are relatively recession-proof.

"We try to avoid buying a little of this or that when we are only lukewarm about the business or its price. When we are convinced as to attractiveness, we believe in buying worthwhile amounts."

Ben Graham

Diversification is powerful - but remember not to overdo it.

"You get recessions, you have stock market declines. If you don't understand that's going to happen, then you're not ready, you won't do well in the markets."

Peter Lynch

Keep in mind the fluidity of the market and the inherent changes. Don't stress too much about short-term declines. Remember the stock market is a long-term investment.

"The stock market is a device for transferring money from the impatient to the patient."

Warren Buffett

Patience, patience, patience. You won't make your fortune overnight - you have to learn to take small losses in stride and focus on the long-term.

"An important key to investing is to remember that stocks are not lottery tickets."

Peter Lynch

The stock market won't make you rich overnight. But then, you have a much higher probability of earning money in the stock market than in the lottery.

"Take charge of your financial future. I believe investing small amounts each month in the stock market will give you financial freedom in the later years of your life."

Bo Sanchez

As we have before, look ahead to the years after you leave your 9-5 job and begin to live the life you deserve! Consistent investments over time will feel like less of a sacrifice and maintaining the habit will compound your earnings.

"Only buy something that you'd be perfectly happy to hold if the market shut down for ten years."

Warren Buffett

We simply can't overemphasize the important of thinking long-term in your investments. Don't buy stocks in the next hot trend if you don't see the company as having true staying power.

"Learn every day, but especially from the experiences of others. It's cheaper!"

John Bogle

Take advantage of the resources available to you to avoid the mistakes others have made and capitalize on strategies that have been proven effective by the best in the field!

"Price is what you pay. Value is what you get."

Warren Buffett

Don't be tempted to load up on only the least expensive stocks. Remember to pay attention to the value of the company and think about it's staying power. As the saying goes, you get what you pay for.

"In many ways, the stock market is like the weather in that if you don't like the current conditions, all you have to do is wait a while."

Low Simpson

One thing you can absolutely count on is that there will be constant change. Again, patience is your best virtue in the stock market. Do your best to wait out the storm and be rewarded at the end of the rainbow.

"In the business world, the rear-view mirror is always cleaner than the windshield."

Warren Buffett

Isn't this just true of life in general? Don't beat yourself up, thinking you should have predicted your losses. Hindsight, as they say, is 20/20. And the stock market, like life, is inherently unpredictable.

"You have to know what you own, and why you own it."

Peter Lynch

Remember to do your own homework. Always know what you're invested in. And keep in mind your *why*.

"Individuals who cannot master their emotions are ill-suited to profit from the investment process."

Benjamin Graham

If you are an overly-anxious person, investment in the stock market may prove emotionally difficult for you. There are many unknowns and a great deal of patience is required to meet you investment goals.

"The game of life is the game over everlasting learning. At least it is if you want to win."

Charlie Munger

You can never stop learning! Always, always, always seek out new knowledge that will lead to better future investments.

"Everyone has the power to follow the stock market. If you made it through fifth grade math, you can do it."

Peter Lynch

As we discussed before, there is a plethora of terminology and it can seem very complicated, but once you get to know it, understanding the stock market is quite simple.

"It's far better to buy a wonderful company at a fair price than a fair company at a wonderful price."

Warren Buffett

True in life as in stock market investment, it's important to consider quality over quantity. Keep in mind that cost and value are separate when you're making decision about which companies to purchase.

"Without a saving faith in the future, no one would ever invest at all. To be an investor, you must be a believer in a better tomorrow."

Benjamin Graham

Hope for a better future is what investment is all about!

Conclusion

Now that you've finished reading this book, I just want to let you know that you already know so much. What took me six whole months to understand, you just read in the past hour or so. And believe me when I tell you this: You are READY. You already have what it takes to be an investor. All you have to do now is take a step forward by following the steps and guides above.

Having read this book, you should have more confidence in your ability to begin making transactions in the stock market. You should know where to find quality advice and some basic terminology that will help you successfully navigate whichever online brokerage firm you choose to use. Your journey in stock market investing is new. But remember to trust yourself and your instincts. Do your homework and get to know and understand the companies you're part-owner in. Make a plan for what to do with dividends. Will you cash them out and treat yourself to something special, or reinvest them so that you can capitalize on those gains? You should now know what are reasons you find good enough to invest in a company, as well as what reasons you may find to sell stock in one. You have your goals set and all that's left to do is commit. This is an exciting time! Don't forget to enjoy the journey to financial freedom! And don't be afraid to dream of the amazing future you can have!

With that, I'd like to ask a little something from you. I would like for you to read the words below aloud. It may sound corny - but do it anyway. These words summarize who you have become in the process of reading this book (and well, it's also an awesome way of ending the book too!) So are you ready? Let's say this all together now.

"I am no longer a slave to money. I am free.

I am no longer a spender, and I am better than a saver.

I am an investor. And I make my money work hard for me!"

P.S. I enjoyed writing this book, and I hope you enjoyed reading it too. Please feel free to share